Between Speech and Silence

POSTMODERN ETHICS SERIES

Postmodernism and deconstruction are usually associated with a destruction of ethical values. The volumes in the Postmodern Ethics series demonstrate that such views are mistaken because they ignore the religious element that is at the heart of existential-postmodern philosophy. This series aims to provide a space for thinking about questions of ethics in our times. When many voices are speaking together from unlimited perspectives within the postmodern labyrinth, what sort of ethics can there be for those who believe there is a way through the dark night of technology and nihilism beyond exclusively humanistic offerings? The series invites any careful exploration of the postmodern and the ethical.

Series Editors:

Marko Zlomislic (Conestoga College)
† David Goicoechea (Brock University)

Other Volumes in the Series:

Cross and Khôra: Deconstruction and Christianity in the Work of John D. Caputo edited by Neal DeRoo and Marko Zlomislić

Agape and Personhood with Kierkegaard, Mother, and Paul (A Logic of Reconciliation from the Shamans to Today) by David Goicoechea

The Poverty of Radical Orthodoxy edited by Lisa Isherwood and Marko Zlomislić

Theologies of Liberation in Palestine-Israel: Indigenous, Contextual, and Postcolonial Perspectives edited by Nur Masalha and Lisa Isherwood

Agape and the Four Loves with Nietzsche, Father, and Q (A Physiology of Reconciliation from the Greeks to Today) by David Goicoechea

Fundamentalism and Gender: Scripture—Body—Community edited by Ulrike Auga, Christina von Braun, Claudia Bruns, and Jana Husmann

Between Speech and Silence

From Communication to Meditation

STEPHEN J. COSTELLO

POSTMODERN ETHICS SERIES 12

☞PICKWICK *Publications* · Eugene, Oregon

BETWEEN SPEECH AND SILENCE
From Communication to Meditation

Postmodern Ethics Series 12

Pickwick Publications
An Imprint of Wipf and Stock Publishers
199 W. 8th Ave., Suite 3
Eugene, OR 97401

www.wipfandstock.com

PAPERBACK ISBN: 978-1-6667-3015-9
HARDCOVER ISBN: 978-1-6667-2128-7
EBOOK ISBN: 978-1-6667-2129-4

Cataloguing-in-Publication data:

Names: Costello, Stephen J., author.

Title: Between speech and silence : from communication to meditation / by Stephen J. Costello.

Description: Eugene, OR: Pickwick Publications, 2022 | Postmodern Ethics Series 12 | Includes bibliographical references and index.

Identifiers: ISBN 978-1-6667-3015-9 (paperback) | ISBN 978-1-6667-2128-7 (hardcover) | ISBN 978-1-6667-2129-4 (ebook)

Subjects: LCSH: Rhetoric. | Dialectic. | Signs and symbols. | Communication. | Silence. | Meditation.

Classification: P99.5 C67 2021 (print) | P99.5 (ebook)

09/15/22

I dedicate this book to Sam Seary in friendship.

The only true wisdom is in knowing that you know nothing.

—Socrates

A prudent question is one-half of wisdom.

—Francis Bacon

At the end of reasons comes persuasion.

—Ludwig Wittgenstein

It is wise to persuade people to do things and make them think it was their own idea.

—Nelson Mandela

Only someone who is silent is listening. And only the invisible is transparent. To be sure, a deeper silence than mere abstention from speech and utterance is required. There is also interior speech which must also become mute, so things might find their proper utterance.

—Josef Pieper

Words without thoughts never to heaven go.

—William Shakespeare

Give every man thy ear, but few thy voice.

—William Shakespeare

Contents

Acknowledgments

I WOULD LIKE TO thank my family, especially my parents, Val and Johnny, for their interest in my work and their incredible enthusiasm and ongoing support, for which I am eternally grateful. My friends, especially Darren Cleary, Derek Smyth, Tom O'Connor, and Sam Seary, to whom I dedicate this book, have also listened in patience to my ideas, provisional titles, and book content over more years than they would care to remember! Their advice was always welcome and much appreciated. I have also learnt much from the counsel, guidance, knowledge, and good company of Mary and Michael Telford, Michael Ryan (our many fruitful and hugely enjoyable conversations), Mary Delaney, and Valerie McGeough. My heartfelt thanks to you all for your availability and kindness.

Introduction

> "The deepest level of communication is not communication,
> but communion . . . It is beyond speech; it is beyond concept
> . . . we are already one. But we imagine that we are not. And
> what we have to recover is our original unity. What we have
> to be is what we are." —Thomas Merton

Preliminary Remarks

We can distinguish *three* disciplines:

1. Thought
2. Speech
3. Action

According to the *Bhagavad Gita*, the *three* gateways to hell are lust, anger, and greed. We can avoid these if we synchronize our thoughts, deeds, and speech, ensuring that we live ethically, mindfully. What the *Gita* calls "austerity of speech" consists in speaking truly, kindly, and helpfully, avoiding words that offend. Putting that another way, speech, which is our subject here, should be:

- Truthful
- Pleasant
- Beneficial

This is the speech that gives no offense. These three need to be aligned so that a one-to-one correspondence is produced between:

- Thought and Speech
- Speech and Action
- Action and Thought

The Story of Helen Keller

At 19 months old, Helen Keller (1880–1968), the American author and activist, became deaf and blind from an unknown illness. She was the first deafblind person to earn a Bachelor of Arts degree and become a lecturer. In her biography, *The Story of My Life*, she recounts how she was given the gift of language from her teacher, Anne Sullivan:

> As the cool stream gushed over one hand, she spelled into the other the word water, first slowly, then rapidly. I stood still, my whole attention fixed upon the motions of her fingers. Suddenly I felt a misty consciousness of something forgotten—a thrill of returning thought; and somehow the mystery of language was revealed to me, I knew then that 'w-a-t-e-r' meant the wonderful cool something that was flowing over my hand. That living word awakened my soul, gave it light, hope, joy, set it free! There were barriers still, it is true, but barriers that could in time be swept away.[1]

Helen Keller later learned five languages.

The Stream of Consciousness in James Joyce

Stream of consciousness is a narrative mode or method that tries to depict the multitudinous thoughts and feelings which pass through the mind of a narrator. We see it deployed in James Joyce, Proust, and Virginia Woolf. In *The Principles of Psychology* (1989), William James describes consciousness as "nothing joined", as something which "flows." A river and a stream are the metaphors by which it is naturally described. *"In talking of it hereafter, let's call it the stream of thought, or consciousness, or subjective life."*[2] But

---

1. https://digital.library.upenn.edu/women/keller/life/life.html.
2. https://genius.com/William-james-chapter-ix-1-the-stream-of-thought-annotated.

it was Joyce who employed it with such startlingly originality in *Ulysees* (1922). Witness this passage where Molly seeks sleep:

> a quarter after what an unearthly hour I suppose therefore just getting up in China now combing out their pigtails for the day well soon have the nuns ringing the angelus theyve nobody coming in to spoil their sleep except an odd priest or two for his night office the alarmlock next door at cockshout clattering the brains out of itself let me see if I can doze off 12345 what kind of flowers are those they invented like the stars the wallpaper in Lombard street was much nicer the apron he gave me was like that something only I only wrote it twice better lower this lamp and try again so that I can get up early.[3]

Samuel Beckett, influenced by Joyce, continued experimenting with words, language and silence in the most minimalist way, his style approaching that of telegraphese. "The sun shone, having no alternative on the nothing new" (*Murphy*). Both these Irish writers sought innovative ways to implode speech, to deconstruct and demolish certainties associated with language and meaning.

Speech and Language

Language may be defined as the method of human communication, be it spoken or written, which consists of the use of words in a conventional sense. Spoken language predates written language by tens of thousands of years. Philosophers in antiquity always privileged this oral tradition.

---

3. https://www.gutenberg.org/files/4300/4300-h/4300-h.htm#chap18

Tepantitla mural in Mexico (circa second century), showing a person emitting a speech scroll from his mouth, symbolising speech. Source: Wiki Commons.

"Cuneiform" is the first known form of written language. It was invented by Sumerians in ancient Mesopotamia, the earliest known civilisation (modern day Southern Iraq), which emerged during the Chalcolithic and early Bronze Ages, between the sixth and fifth millennium BC. Cuneiform derives from the Latin *cuneus* meaning "wedge." These were wedge-shaped marks on clay tablets made by means of a blunt reed for a stylus (a small writing tool/utensil).

Linguistics is the scientific study of language. Key thinkers here include Ferdinand de Saussure and Noam Chomsky, but the philosophy of language began with Plato in Ancient Greece, with his dialogue, the *Gorgias*. Philosophers in the twentieth century such as Ludwig Wittgenstein and Jacques Derrida would make the study of language central to their thought. Jean-Jacques Rousseau argued that language originated from emotions, while Immanuel Kant asserted it came from rational thought.

There are approximately 5,000 to 7,000 languages in the world. Natural languages are spoken or signed—speaking, writing, whistling, braille (a tactile writing system used by the visually impaired). All languages rely on the process of semiosis to relate signs to meaning. *Lingua* in Latin means "language" or "tongue." Many thinkers have been associated with semiotics, such as Charles Sanders Peirce and Umberto Eco, to name but two. A sign is anything that communicates a meaning, that is not the sign itself, to the interpreter of the signs. The meaning can be intentional or unintentional. Hermeneutics is the philosophical and theological art of interpretation (of texts etc.) and names associated with this discipline include Hans-Georg Gadamer, Martin Heidegger, and Paul Ricoeur.

Language is processed in the Boca's and Wernickie's areas of the brain. Language's origins began when early hominids started gradually changing their primate communication system, acquiring the ability to form a theory of other minds and a shared intentionality (representation). Oral languages contain a phonological system that governs how symbols are used to form sequences known as words. Humans acquire language through social interaction in early childhood and children speak fluently by the age of three. Languages evolve—they are living systems. The Indo-European family is the most widely spoken. If *langue* is the language system, *parole* (word) is the speech in a particular language. Plato held that communication is possible because language represents ideas and concepts that exist prior to and independent of language. Speech is the expression of thoughts and feelings through discourse—articulate sounds (combinations of vowels and consonants), which the larynx produces. The formal study of language is considered to have begun in ancient India—a subcontinent with a 3,500-year-old history. Sanskrit is the liturgical language of Hinduism.

Humans have speculated about the origins of language throughout history. The biblical myth of the Tower of Babel is one such account. Genesis 11:1–9 is an origin myth meant to explain why the world's peoples speak different languages.

The Tower of Babel by Pieter Bruegel the Elder (1563). Source: Wiki Commons.

The story tells of a united race in the generations following the Great Flood who spoke a single language and migrated Westward where they built a city and a tower tall enough to reach Heaven. God, however, compounds their speech so they can no longer understand each other and scatters them. *Babel* in Hebrew means "to jumble" or "to confuse." In English, we say "the babble of a brook" (meaning the continuous murmuring of flowing sound) and "to babble" (meaning to talk rapidly or foolishly). It's an appealing myth: that early humanity spoke a single language.

Rhetoric and Dialectic

All of us are confronted countless times each day with the challenge of communicating with, or persuading, others. In an age of inane information, slogans, soundbites, and short attention span, communicating lucidly and intelligibly has arguably never been more important. What is the secret of being able to communicate with clarity and convince with credibility? Are there techniques, tools or tricks that can be taught? The answer is in the affirmative.

A field of psychoanalytic psychology called "Transactional Analysis," which was developed by Eric Berne in the late 1950's, has identified *four* largely unconscious ways of communicating with others. We can communicate as:

1. Adult-to-Adult
2. Child-to-Adult
3. Child-to-Child
4. Adult-to-Child

The Art of Persuasion, by contrast, was refined more than 2,000 years ago in ancient Greece. We will explore the Socratic method of open enquiry as well as the timeless art of what the ancient philosophers called 'rhetoric', with its three-fold secret of *ethos*, *logos*, and *pathos*. I will outline, in what follows, some core *philosophical* and *practical* principles and effective communication strategies which are the key to success in preparing a presentation, delivering a speech, negotiating a business deal, writing an essay, winning an argument, advertising a product, or selling an item.

Aside from the stratagems and skills of rhetoric, the Socratic Method of examination will be outlined. which assumes the form of cooperative dialogue based on asking and answering questions to stimulate critical thinking and draw out underlying presuppositions, and which can be applied in almost any situation in which one finds oneself. Our aim is to show how character (integrity) and truth are ultimately the best persuaders in dialogue and debate; how important it is to really listen and pay attention in conversation; how we can practically apply the lessons of the great philosophers to our everyday negotiations, pitching, selling, speech-making, writing, etc., rather than simply relying, as important as they are, on the tools and tactics of rhetoric—in short, to show that wisdom is more important than winning.

> "The aim of argument, or of discussion, should not be victory,
> but progress", Joseph Joubert

Chapter 1 will cover the core principles and practices of rhetoric. Our philosopher-guides here will be Aristotle, Cicero, Schopenhauer, and Daniel Dennett, a contemporary philosopher. In chapter 2, I will discuss the Socratic Method (dialectic) in some detail, with reference to Plato. Taken together, they teach us *how to convince through debate and converse through dialogue*. Chapter 3 will issue in a shift of gear as we proceed to explore the importance of stories and symbolism. Chapter 4 will highlight the nine speaking styles with reference to the Enneagram system. In chapter 5, I set out the principles of compassionate communication. Finally, chapter 6 considers the role of silence and the practice of meditation, when all speech stops, largely but not exclusively from the perspective of Advaita Vedanta. In the Appendix, I adumbrate Jacques Lacan's psychoanalytic discourse theory. The carefully selected quotations throughout serve as place-holders for contemplation. This book is, in a nutshell, about *three* things: conversing, convincing, and communing with one's Self in stillness and silence. It links with two other works of mine—*Dynamics of Discernment* and *The Nine Faces of Fear*—providing thematic coherence and thus, to an extent, constituting a trilogy.

If the silent voice is inaudible, mute, and ineffective, the shrill voice is vociferous, raucous and clamours hysterically for attention. What is needed most of all in society is the sane voice, which is rational, reasonable, and as sensible as it is sapiential. It is my hermeneutic hope that this voice prevails both in this book and in the wider world. We are in much need of it.

1

The Art of Rhetoric

"Character may almost be called the most effective
means of persuasion."—Aristotle

"The fool tells me his reasons. The wise man
persuades me with my own.—Aristotle

Rhetoric vs Socratic Method

More Flies are Caught with Honey than with Vinegar

IN THIS CHAPTER, WE will consider rhetoric (debate), while the following chapter will cover dialectic (dialogue). Both rhetoric and dialectic presuppose a situation of conflict, where two contradictory responses can be given. It is the interlocutor who must be persuaded. Through the use of skillful questions, a game of intellectual joust or gymnastics occurs. Socrates asks questions—he does not provide answers as he purports to know nothing. Both these disciplines invite someone to a philosophical conversion, to a metamorphosis, a transformation of one's way of living and thinking through the psychagogic power of language. One's natural attitude is suspended (placed in *epochê* or brackets). The experience of being on the receiving end of the "Socratic situation" is akin to being stung by darts, with small, sharp interrogations. For Aristotle, these two disciplines were techniques of persuasion; for Plato, by contrast, philosophy was essentially dialectic—a common, universal search for the Truth. As such, dialectic was a spiritual exercise. It was Aristotle, who first formulated the art of rhetoric in a systematic sense. For Socrates, rhetoric was, "Not an art at all, but the habit of a bold and ready wit, which knows how to manage mankind: this habit I sum up under the word "flattery."" Socrates argued that rhetoric should always be in the service of virtue, especially justice. Socrates's particular method is employed to uncover wisdom, knowledge, and lasting truth.

> "The aim is to uncover the truth, not just win an argument.
> This is a joint endeavor." —Plato

Origin and History of Rhetoric

The origin of rhetoric as a subject was Mesopotamia in ancient Egypt, a society who held speaking in high regard. In ancient China, rhetoric dates back to Confucius (551–479 BC). In ancient Greece, the earliest mention of rhetoric occurs in Homer's *Iliad*. Rhetoric may be defined as the art of persuasion. It's one of *three* ancient arts. Aristotle defined rhetoric as "the faculty of observing in any given case the available means of persuasion." Mastery of this art was seen as essential in the law courts, in the assembly and in civic ceremonies. From ancient Greece to the late 19th century, rhetoric played a central role in Western education in training orators, lawyers, and statesmen. Plato, however, criticized the "Sophists" who were well-paid, popular professionals (hence our English word, "sophistry," used pejoratively) for using rhetoric as a means of deceit (teaching, for example, how a weak argument could defeat a strong one with all the tricks of the trade) instead of discovering truth. In the dialogue, *Gorgias*, Plato defines rhetoric as the persuasion of ignorant masses. Plato viewed rhetoric with suspicion. If knowledge concerns itself with what is commonly regarded as "truth," rhetoric, he argued, concerned itself with the *effects* of statements on the audience thus degenerating into "empty speak," ultimately reflecting an indifference to truth. Basically, Plato regarded rhetoric as a form of flattery which functions a bit like cookery—masking the undesirability of unhealthy food by making it taste good. Aristotle redeemed rhetoric and extended its scope to include any appropriate means of persuasion in a given situation. Throughout European history, rhetoric has concerned itself with persuasion in public and political settings. Rhetoric flourishes in open democratic societies with rights of free speech. In short, rhetoric is a civic art with the power to shape characters and communities, when employed correctly. Cicero, the Roman orator, trusted rhetoric to support the republic. He argued that the art required ethics as much as eloquence. In other words, a good orator needed also to be a good man—an enlightened person on a wide variety of topics. Rhetoric was later taught in the universities during the Middle Ages as one of the three (*trivium*) liberal arts, together with Logic and Grammar, after which it declined before being resurrected in the 18th century when it assumed a more social role with the rise of elocution schools. In the 20th century, rhetoric developed as a field of study in schools and colleges with courses in public speaking and Communication Studies. Indeed, rhetoric was and continues to be part of the curriculum of many Jesuit centers of learning. History has seen the rehabilitation of (Aristotelian) rhetoric, as a counterpart to (Socratic) dialectic.

The Three Types of Rhetoric

According to Aristotle, there are *three* types (*genres*) of civic rhetoric:

1. **Forensic** (judicial)—truth or falsity of events that took place in the past; issues of guilt (courtroom).

2. **Deliberative** (political)—determining whether actions should be taken or not in the future (making laws).

3. **Epideictic** (ceremonial)—praise or blame; demonstrating beauty or skill (eulogy or wedding toast).

Aristotle understood rhetoric as *techne*—a technical skill which could be learnt and practiced. He argued that *three* characteristics were needed for persuasion: intelligence, virtue, and goodwill. Teaching the persuasive aspects of any subject matter was rhetoric. "Let rhetoric be the power to observe the persuasiveness of which any particular matter admits," is the opening statement of Aristotle's *The Art of Rhetoric*. Oratorical confidence was seen as an essential asset for politicians in the Athenian Assemblies and Councils, and for the citizens in the courts of law. Aristotle's *Rhetoric* goes far deeper, though, than merely presenting debaters' tricks. Aristotle established the methods of critical, informal reasoning. He also offered a detailed discussion on the psychology of character and the emotions, on friendship and happiness. Persuasiveness, under Aristotle, became a scientific exercise which could be taught but only against the background of a knowledge of human nature.

The Five Principles of Rhetoric

The *five* canons of rhetoric, i.e., phases for developing a persuasive speech, as set out by Aristotle in his *The Art of Rhetoric* (335 BC), are: invention (*inventio*), arrangement (*dispositio*), style (*elocutio*), memory (*memoria*) and delivery (*actio*).

1. Invention

Invention is concerned with identifying the central questions that lie at the heart of the issue being addressed and marshalling the most persuasive arguments to answer it. The answer may be witnesses or contracts or through rhetorical devices by which the speaker builds an argument based on *ethos* (character), *logos* (reasoning) and *pathos* (passion)—the *three* persuasive audience appeals.

2. Arrangement

Arrangement is about how to structure and order an argument. It asks: what's the strongest point? In what way should the case be made? It's the thinking and organizing framework for the case's presentation.

3. Style

Style involves choosing the most persuasive and evocative language to make your case. It's the way you express yourself—the choice of words (diction) and how you put them into sentences (composition). There are grand, middle and plain styles. Metaphor (expressing something in terms of something else) may be employed as well as humor: wit and wisdom so.

4. Memory

Memory refers to memorizing speeches. Only write a few key sentences or words on a prompt card. Rather than fixating on recalling what you've learnt, focus instead on getting the thrust (key points) of your message across.

5. Delivery

This is about aligning your (control of) voice and body language (gestures) with your message. Non-verbal communication reveals your emotional state. Your body and words must say the same thing. It's not *what* you say, it's *how* you say it. A good message can get a bad presentation; poor content can be made to sound appealing, by means of an excellent presentation. Thus, combine style with substance. These five principles can be deployed in business presentations, debating, selling, communicating, or negotiating.

Aristotelian Advice

1. Your own material should be amplified

2. The case of an adversary should be diminished

3. A summary or recapitulation may be appropriate

4. The speech should end inspiring emotion

   "I have spoken, you have heard, you have the facts, judge." — Aristotle

Five-Point Presentation

1. *Exordium* is the bait—a story or statement which arouses the interest of an audience. This comes at the beginning of a speech.

2. *Narratio* is the problem or question—you pose a problem or a question that has to be solved or answered. It is the narrative account.

3. *Confirmatio* or the solution/answer—you resolve the issue that has been raised. The appeal to *logos* is emphasized in this, the main body of the speech.

4. *Refutatio* is the payoff or benefit—you state specific advantages to each member of the audience for adopting the course of action recommended. The refutation answers counterarguments.

5. *Peroratio* is a call to action—you state the concrete steps/actions required to follow, through *pathos*.

Structure of a Presentation

Your story will shift from the specific to the general and back to the specific. The problem is such and such. What is the solution? What is the payoff/ advantage of adopting this solution? What I am asking you to do is such and such. The call to action is more powerful when it is concrete (should always be concrete). The solution should be no more than three points. The final stage of preparation is creating a bait. This is prepared last but presented first. The best baits are stories from personal experience. (Use metaphors and symbols or present a shocking statistic).

Format for Answering Questions

It's not enough to make an effective/powerful presentation if you then fail to answer pertinent questions! Follow this *three-point-process*:

1. *Point*—this is the one point or statement you want to make in reply to the question.

2. *Reason*—this is the one supporting argument for the point. After stating your point, you say, "That's because . . . " or "The reason is . . . ."

3. *Example*—this is the example or brief story that illustrates the point you have made.

Cost Benefit

How do you effectively answer questions? The answer should always be stated in terms of BENEFIT. Stick to the structure: point, reason, example. Some people have a way with words. Language must be persuasive (create word pictures; employ metaphors; humor; storytelling; both brains, e.g., left brain analytical, literal, logical, and right brain creative, visual, holistic, metaphorical etc.). A saying attributed to Confucius: "I hear, and I forget. I see and I remember. I do and I understand." Image + Feeling = Memory.

The Three-Step Sequence

Employ the three-step sequence. You can persuade through the use of *logos, pathos, ethos*—the *three* steps in rhetoric we mentioned above. Speak or write from your head, your heart, and your soul. These three are the character of the speaker, the disposition of the audience, and the speech itself. Three factors in every speech include the speaker, the subject, and the listener.

Ethos

Logos   *Pathos*

Ethos or Character

Ethos is the character (ethical integrity) of the person. Character connotes constancy. Your reputation is everything. Who are you? What do you stand for? What are your values and beliefs? Why should I trust you? Make your word your bond. Be on the level. What added value do you bring to the discussion? *Ethos* builds trust and confidence. It is persuasion through character portrayal—the deeds and life of the person. Show your character, so. Stories sell better than facts. Be personal without being intimate. People need to know *who* you are.

Logos or Reasoning

Logos is the Word or Reason or Meaning. It's the work of the head (the left-side of the brain). It's logical reasoning, rational argumentation. *Logos* can proceed through induction or deduction. These are the weapons to win an argument. So, be reasonable and rational. This concerns *what* you're saying. Contradictions and illogicality persuade no-one.

Pathos or Passion

Pathos is argument based on emotional appeal. This is the feeling you have for your subject—the passion that it ignites in you. This is about *how* you're saying it. *Pathos* shows feeling—sympathy or "suffering." It demonstrates how committed you are. It's the work of the heart. It involves the right-side of the brain. Stories convince more than logical reasoning, as we said above. Emerson once remarked that one person with a belief is worth thousands who have only interests. The goal here is to sway the feelings of the listeners so that they will side with you. Genuine passion derives from deep-seated beliefs. These three *taken together* are extremely effective as a tool in any situation which demands persuasion. It's important to get the balance right. For example, a *pathos*-laden speech can be sentimental and saccharine. A *logos*-driven speech can be too heady, boringly factual and lack warmth as well as connection.

We might also mention "refutation" and "peroration." Refutation (*refutatio*) is being able to refute an opponent's arguments. The conclusion or epilogue (*peroratio*) is the climax or *dénouement*. In the final part of the speech (or piece of writing) you should recapitulate or summarize (*précis*) previous points, especially exciting indignation or arousing pity or sympathy for your client or yourself. This is the favorite part of the speech for employing *pathos*. End on a dramatic note. So, keep these three factors in mind when next writing or delivering a persuasive speech and see if you can incorporate and deploy all three. To conclude this section on Aristotle, ask:

- How do you see yourself?
- How do others see you?
- Who do you need to influence?

Prepare for the negotiation; ask:

- What are *your* objectives?
- How can you meet them?
- What are *their* objectives?
- How can they meet them?

Formula: *Question equals brief Answer plus your One agenda point.* $Q = A + 1$. We turn now from Aristotle's advice to Cicero's on the subject of rhetoric.

Cicero

Marcus Tullius Cicero (106–43 BC) was a Roman statesman and one of the most significant rhetoricians of all times. Others include Quintilian, Boethius, Erasmus, Bacon, Hobbes etc. In *How to Win An Argument: An Ancient Guide to the Art of Persuasion*, a "Ciceronian Check Sheet for

Effective Speaking," is given, and I reproduce his ancient practical philosophical advice below.

Ten Guidelines from Cicero

1. **Nature, art** and **practice, practice, practice.** These are the *three* requisites for becoming an effective speaker. The good or excellent speaker possesses certain qualities bestowed by nature such as a pleasant voice ("I could listen to him all day") or perhaps being equipped with the ability to project your voice. Mastery of the art of rhetoric is also essential. One's natural gifts (talents) and knowledge of the rules of rhetoric need to be enhanced by purposeful practice (perfected through repetition, habit, and daily discipline).

2. **Eloquence.** Eloquent speech is a powerful weapon to have in your arsenal. Such stylish speeches can be powerful. Use yours for the betterment rather than the detriment of others.

3. **Identify, arrange, memorize.** When setting out to construct a speech or argument, identify the point at hand; deploy appropriate material for proving it; arrange the material effectively (structure) and strategically; apply a suitable style; commit to memory; and employ a fitting way/manner to deliver it.

4. **Not by logic alone.** To persuade is not simply to argue logically. Recall the three sources of persuasion: a) rational argumentation, b) proof based on character, c) emotional appeal. Cicero recommends the use of all three Aristotelian aspects of persuasion in order to teach, delight, and move an audience. There is a time and a place for each. A syllogism such as "All men are mortal. Socrates is a man. Therefore, Socrates is mortal" might be more appropriate in a philosophy lecture whereas in a debate a better, less boring sentence might be "we play our parts and we die." The skillful speaker will know when to engage with each.

5. **Know your audience.** Context is crucial for the cultivation of different styles of speech. A formal setting with strangers is different from an informal gathering of friends. It's important to keep this in mind when composing and choosing the various words for your speech. Adapt your speech according to the particular occasion and to the audience that's being addressed.

6. **Be clear, be correct.** Apply the virtues of correctness, clarity, distinction, appropriateness. Ensure you're correct in your spellings and syntax, clear in your argumentation, distinctive in your use of various figures of speech such as metaphor, and appropriate to the time, occasion and audience.

7. **Delivery matters.** Sometimes it's *how* you say it. There are brilliant but boring teachers, just as there are salesmen with no substance. Speak clearly, cogently, and compellingly with voice, gesture, and content.

8. **Imitation** (*mimesis*). Imitation is the sincerest form of flattery. Find good role models to emulate. But be yourself too. Imitate their strengths; don't just copy. You want to be authentic and not just a pale reflection of somebody else.

9. **The pen is mightier than the sword.** Words are weapons too. Use them diligently and mindfully. The pen is a close second to a tongue.

10. **Words without substance are hollow things.** Without solid knowledge as a foundation, the words that flow from a speaker's mouth are just child's prattle. Best to be steeped in literature, law, history, and philosophy—in the liberal arts.

   "Rem tene, verba sequentur": "Grasp the subject, the words will follow."—Cato the Elder

Consider:

- Joining Toastmasters
- Reading, watching, or listening to great speeches, such as:

  - George Washington's Farewell Address, September 7th, 1796
  - Abraham Lincoln's Gettysburg Address, November 19th, 1863
  - Patrick Pearse, "The fools, the fools! They have left us our Fenian dead" speech, August 1st, 1915
  - Winston Churchill's House of Commons speech, May 13th, 1940
  - Franklin D. Roosevelt's Inaugural Address, March 4th, 1933
  - Nelson Mandela's "Free at Last" speech, May 2nd, 1994
  - John F. Kennedy's Inaugural Address, January 20th, 1961

- Martin Luther King Jr's "I have a dream" speech at the Lincoln Memorial in Washington, August 28th, 1963 and his "I've seen the promised land" speech in Memphis, Tennessee, April 3rd, 1968

We now look to a nineteenth-century philosopher—Arthur Schopenhauer—for some more stratagems in the art of rhetoric, which is so apposite in our age of fake news and alt-facts.

The Art of Always Being Right: 38 Subtle Ways of Persuasion

The German philosopher, Arthur Schopenhauer (1788–1860) knew all the tricks of classical rhetoric. He saw it at work in the specious and sophistic arguments of politicians and pretenders of all kinds. In response, he penned his *Art of Being Right*. This tract is full of wit and wisdom and one of the best inoculations against "crooked thinking" that has ever been written.

Socrates and Plato had contempt for the Sophists. The former were concerned with the true and the good—with what they called "dialectic," which for them was the sincere and sustained attempt through open enquiry effected by means of question, answer, and discussion as against the Sophist's use of rhetoric/debate for the purposes merely of persuasion.

Schopenhauer was a serious intellectual and so when he talks of the tricks of rhetoric he is warning *against* these devices in the hands of unscrupulous opponents. So, a certain amount of (Socratic) irony is present in his work. Schopenhauer's tricks of the trade include: making your opponent angry; attacking him rather than his arguments; asking him so many different questions that you confuse him; when he denies a proposition, put it in its converse form so that he affirms it; use subtle distinctions and arcane definitions to discombobulate him; make your opponent agree with a number of true propositions, then assert among them the propositions you wish him to accept; distract your opponent from any line of questioning that may defeat you, by introducing alternative lines of thought to confuse and off-center him.

He begins by saying that the aim of his reflections is to help people come across as right even if they are wrong; conversely, one may be in the right objectively but come off worse in an argument. We need stratagems, therefore (some of these are quite complicated so I have underlined the ones I recommend):

- **Extension**. exaggerate your opponents' position. You will thus make it sound farcical. And keep your own preliminary points narrow/restricted.

- **Homonyms**. Here you extend a proposition to something which has little or nothing in common with the matter in question but the similarity of the word—then refute it triumphantly and so claim credit for having refuted the original statement.

- **Generalize your opponent's specific statements**. Here you take a proposition which is in reference to some particular matter as through it were uttered with a universal application. Aristotle's example: A Moor is black but in regard to his teeth he is white; therefore, he is black and not black at the same time.

What these three tricks above have in common is this: something different is attacked from that which was asserted. Sometimes what the opponent says is true, but it stands in apparent and not in real contradiction with the thesis. So, all that the person whom he is attacking has to do is deny the validity of the conclusion which he draws. Thus, his refutation is itself directly refuted by a denial of his conclusion.

Another trick is to refuse to admit true premises because of a foreseen conclusion.

- **Conceal your game.** Here to get your conclusion accepted, you must not let it be foreseen (shown in advance). Rather, get the premises accepted one by one, unobserved. Or if you think your opponent won't accept your conclusion, get several of the premises accepted. You conceal your strategy as you proceed circuitously.

- **False premises.** To prove the truth of a proposition, you can employ previous presuppositions that are not true, should your opponent refuse to admit the true ones. The plan is to take propositions which are false in themselves but true for your opponent and argue from the way in which he thinks. A true conclusion may follow from false premises but not vice versa. Similarly, your opponent's false propositions may be refuted by other false propositions which he, however, takes to be true.

- **Postulate what has to be proven.** Beg the question in disguise by postulating what has to be proven, either: under another name or by making a general assumption covering the point in dispute.

- **Yield admissions through questions.** He who states the proposition and wants to prove it can proceed against his opponent by question, in order to show the truth of the statement from his opponent's admissions. (The Socratic method, Schopenhauer says is akin to this). The plan here is to ask your opponent a great many, far-reaching questions all at once, so as to hide what you want to get admitted and, on the other hand, quickly propound the argument resulting from his admissions. The gaps are scarcely noticed.

- **Make your opponent angry.** If he is angry, he is incapable of seeing where his advantage lies. "You can make him angry by doing him repeated injustice, or practicing some kind of chicanery, and being generally insolent."[1]

- **Question in detouring order.** Here you put a question in an order different from that which the conclusion to be drawn from it requires and transpose it so as to keep hidden that at which you're aiming. Or use your opponent's answers for different or even opposite conclusions according to their character.

- **Take advantage of the no-sayer.** If you see that your opponent returns a negative answer on purpose to the questions which you want him to answer in the affirmative, you ask the converse of the proposition, as though it were that which you were anxious to see affirmed.

- **Generalize admissions of specific cases.** "If you make an induction, and your opponent grants you the particular cases by which it is to be supported, you must refrain from asking him if he also admits the general truth which issues from the particulars but introduce it afterwards as a settled and admitted fact. In the meanwhile, he will himself come to believe that he has admitted it, and the same impression will be received by the audience."

- **Choose metaphors favorable to your proposition.** If the conversation turns to some general discussion which requires some figurative speech, begin by choosing a metaphor that serves your purposes. "A speaker often betrays his purpose beforehand by the names which he gives to things."

---

1. This and other quotes from Schopenhauer's *The Art of Being Right* can be found at https://en.wikisource.org/wiki/The_Art_of_Being_Right.

- **Agree to reject the counterargument.** To make your opponent accept a proposition, you must give him the counterproposition as well, leaving him his choice of the two. Render the contrast glaring between the two so that to avoid being paradoxical he will accept the proposition, which is made to look quite plausible, probable even. E.g., if you want to make him admit a boy must do everything his father tells him to do, ask whether "in all things we must obey or disobey our parents."

- <u>**Claim victory despite defeat.**</u> When your opponent has answered several of your questions without the answers turning out as you wanted (favorable to the conclusion at which you were aiming) advance the desired conclusion—even though it doesn't in the least follow—as though it had been proved and proclaim it in a tone of triumph! If your opponent is stupid or shy, says Schopenhauer, it just may succeed.

- **Use seemingly absurd propositions.** You could offer some true proposition to your opponent, the truth of which is not palpable as though you wished to draw your proof from it. Should he reject it because he suspects a trick, you can show how absurd he is. Should he accept it, you have reason (momentarily) on your side.

- <u>**Use your opponent's views.**</u> When your opponent advances a proposition see if it is inconsistent with some other proposition he has admitted. E.g., if he defends suicide, you may exclaim, "Why don't you hang yourself?," even if it's "claptrap," as Schopenhauer says!

- **Defense through subtle distinction.** If your opponent corners you with a counterproof, you may be able to advance a subtle distinction especially if the discussion is ambiguous anyway.

- <u>**Interrupt, break-up, divert the debate.**</u> If you are about to lose the debate, you mustn't allow your opponent to continue on his course of argument, but interrupt him, break the discussion off, derail it, lead him away from the subject, deflect his attention. Change the discussion!

- **Generalize the matter, then argue against it.** Should your opponent challenge you to produce any objection to some particular point on which you have nothing to say, turn the discussion towards more general matters.

- **Draw conclusions yourself.** When all the premises have been elicited, don't ask your opponent for the conclusion. Rather, draw it out yourself, especially in case the premises had been lacking somewhat.

- **Counter with an argument as bad as his.** If your opponent offers a superficial argument, then it's best to meet that with a counterargument which is just as superficial as his! "For it is with victory that you are concerned, not with truth," Schopenhauer writes.

- **Beg the question.** If your opponent requires you to admit some point which follows from a premise, simply refuse to do so, declaring that he is begging the question. Deprive him of his best argument!

- **Make him exaggerate.** Contradiction and contention irritate and annoy a person into exaggerating their claims. By contradicting and goading him thus, you may drive him into extending beyond the limits of the discussion or of what he knows. You then refute the exaggerated form of it as though you had refuted the original statement. Be careful that you yourself aren't caught in the same snare.

- **State a false syllogism.** "Your opponent puts forward a proposition, and by false inference and distortion of his ideas you force from its other propositions which it does not contain, and he does not in the least mean."

- **Find one instance to the contrary.** This is a case of diversion. When many propositions are offered, simply divert to one instance to which the proposition does not apply, and it will be overthrown.

- **Turn the tables.** Here, you turn your opponent's argument against himself.

- **Anger indicates a weak point.** Should your opponent surprise you by getting angry, urge it on with even more zeal. It's a good thing to make him angry especially as you've probably detected his weak point.

- **Persuade the audience, not the opponent.** If you have no refutation on offer, you can make one aimed at the audience instead. You can start an invalid objection which only the academic or expert knows is invalid. Usually, you can add insult to injury by getting some laughs from the audience. Play to the gallery.

- **Diversion.** If you find your argument is collapsing you can make a diversion, as though it had a bearing on the matter, and afforded an argument against your opponent! This is ameliorated if you personalize the nature of the diversion.

- **Appeal to authority rather than reason.** Make appeals to authority especially if your opponent may not have any knowledge of. You can weigh him (down) with many such arguments. You can also twist your authorities, falsify them or quote something you yourself have invented. You could also employ universal opinion as authority. Things can easily be distorted to suit your side of the debate (especially in the case of statistics).

- **This is beyond me.** If you have no reply to your opponent, you could just say with irony, "This eludes my poor powers of comprehension. It may be true, but I just can't understand what he's getting at. I must refrain from expressing an opinion on the matter until I am equipped with more facts at my disposal." You could gesture and exclaim, "I don't think any of us here present can follow the thread of your argument." Or ask him to provide you with examples and particular cases or keep asking what he means by such and such. Feign stupidity or naivety.

- **Put his thesis into some odious category.** Throw suspicion on an assertion by putting it into some odious category, even though the connection is only apparent. You can say something like, "That's a form of Manicheanism." Or you can say, "you're committing a category mistake as we say in philosophy" or state that the system/theory in question has been refuted years ago.

- **It applies in theory, but not in practice.** You can say, "That's all very well in theory but it won't work in practice." Here you admit the premise but deny the conclusion. You imply that what's wrong in practice is wrong in theory too.

- **Don't let him off the hook.** If your opponent doesn't give you a direct answer, don't let him off the hook. Watch out for evasions and counter-questions because you have touched on a weak spot. In these cases, urge the point all the more. Go in for the kill, even if you aren't completely sure yourself where the weakness you have hit upon really lies.

- **Will is more effective than insight.** Here instead of working on your opponent's intellect by knowledge, you work on his will by motive. Will is more effective than insight and intelligence. Schopenhauer's example: a clergyman is defending some philosophical dogma; you make him realize it's in contradiction with one of the dogmas of his Christian faith and he abandons it immediately.

- **The Vicar of Wakefield.** (This is the name of a novel by Oliver Goldsmith that turns in this type of persuasion). You puzzle your opponent by bombast that seems very deep. Schopenhauer remarks: "It is a well-known fact that in recent times some philosophers [Hegel no doubt!] have practiced this trick on the whole of the public with the most brilliant success."

- **A faulty proof refutes his whole position.** Should your opponent be in the right but choose a faulty proof you can easily manage to refute it and then claim you have refuted his whole position.

- <u>**The ultimate strategy.**</u> The last trick is to become personal, insulting, rude, as soon as you see that your opponent is gaining the upper hand and that you are coming off worst. Here you leave the argument and center your attention on the person of your opponent. It's best to carry this out in a quiet and calm demeanor, because this will enrage him all the more. If your opponent becomes personal, merely say, "That has no bearing on this discussion." Take no notice of his insults as you continue to show him that he is wrong.

Schopenhauer concludes his little book commending us to appeal to reason and to cherish truth and to be just enough to bear being proved wrong. Schopenhauer says that scarcely one man in a hundred is worth your disputing with him so let the remainder say what they like "for everyone is at liberty to be a fool." Sometimes peace is better than truth. As one proverb reminds us: "peace hangs on the tree of silence." Basically, there's no argument to "yes!" Or simply abide by the maxim: "don't negotiate with terrorists," who come in all shapes and sizes.

A Contemporary Account

The twentieth-century American philosopher, Daniel Dennett, follows the classical trivium deriving from Aristotle's division of thought into Logic, Grammar, and Rhetoric in his *Intuition Pumps and Other Tools for Thinking*. He maintains it matters:

a. how we arrive at our ideas

b. how we express them

    c. how we treat the people with whom we converse,
       especially those with whom we disagree.

Rhetoric has come to mean false or flattering speech, but Dennett wants to return it to its original meaning as being more akin to kindness. Thus, rhetoric as eloquent, ethical, and emotional sensitivity. There are *four* steps to his rhetorical rules.

Four Rhetorical Rules

1. Try to re-express your opponent's position so clearly and frankly that they will thank you for it, wishing they could have put it that way.

2. List any points of agreement.

3. Mention anything you've learned from your opponent.

4. Only then are you allowed to say so much as a word of criticism or rebuttal.

This, then, is Dennett's strategy—only when we fully understand an opponent's position as well as they do, can we participate in a shared ethos by finding points of agreement; there is no point alienating one's opponent. We must, rather, try to understand an opposing position. This greatly helps one presenting one's own case. We must proceed by way of response rather than reaction in a respectful discussion. Here are his *seven* tools for critical thinking.

Seven Rules for Critical Thinking

1. Use your mistakes: from every obstacle comes an opportunity.

2. Respect your opponent. Don't be pedantic or pompous. You want to *persuade* people. So, seek to understand your opponent's position.

3. Beware of the "Surely" klaxon (electric horn). Treat the word "surely" as a rhetorical warning sign that someone employs without offering sufficient evidence or reason. It signals a weak spot in their argument.

4. Answer rhetorical questions. A rhetorical question can be a substitute for thinking. Even if the answer is obvious, state it anyway.

5. Deploy "Occam's Razor" ("entities should not be multiplied without necessity"). This is the law/principle of parsimony—don't concoct or complicate a theory when a simpler one will do.

6. Sturgeon's Law, which states that "90% of everything is crap." Don't waste time on rubbish, i.e., on arguments that aren't any good. No axe-grinding!

7. Beware of "Deepities." A "deepity" is a proposition that seems important and true/profound but achieves this effect by being ambiguous.

Start with Why

Finally, in *Start with Why: How Great Leaders Inspire Everyong to Take Action*, Simon Sinek elaborates on what he calls The Golden Circle, which consists of WHAT, HOW and WHY. WHAT we do are the services we provide; HOW we do it is our unique selling point/proposition (USP); WHY we do it is our belief system. To put it another way: WHAT is the result, HOW are the actions, WHY is the cause. This is his diagram:

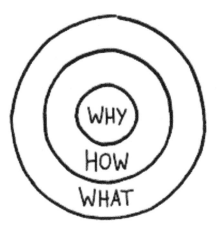

Source: Sinek, *Start with Why*.

We can describe these *three* degrees of certainty thus:

WHY: Purpose

HOW: Principles

WHAT: Products

Success, according to Sinek, is the result of pursuing WHY (our purpose). Inspired leaders communicate and convince from the inside out. They begin with WHY. He gives the example of what a marketing message from Apple might look like (if they were like everyone else):

> "We make great computers.
>
> They're beautifully designed, simple to use and user-friendly.
>
> Wanna buy one?"

Now start with WHY:

> "Everything we do, we believe in challenging the status quo.
> We believe in thinking differently.
>
> The way we challenge the status quo is by making our products beautifully designed, simple to use and user-friendly.
>
> And we happen to make great computers.
>
> Wanna buy one?"

Sinek's central contention is: *People don't buy WHAT you do, they buy WHY you do it.* "Why" is philosophical; "what" and "how" are practical. It's the *belief* not the *brand* that inspires loyalty. The Golden Circle is more than a communications hierarchy; it corresponds/correlates with levels of the brain:

WHAT: Neocortex

HOW and WHY: Limbic System

WHY must come first—it's the emotional component of desire and decision-making. Convincing is ultimately about winning hearts and minds—precisely in that order. People need to believe in something bigger than themselves—in a cause or call (self-transcendence). Each piece/part of The Golden Circle must be in balance, aligned, in right order. All three must be clear, coherent, and consistent. WHAT and HOW you do things must be in congruence with your WHY. Concentrate on WHY then HOW you will do it. If HOWs are the values, WHY is the vision. If you don't know WHY, you can't know HOW.

In the USA, the WHY is the "American Dream"—there is a culture code (fit). WHY changes how we do things. WHY is compelling. To be moved by Why is to be motivated by meaning. Sinek says that Dr Martin Luther King gave the world his famous "I have a Dream" speech that mobilized a nation; it wasn't "I have a Plan" speech! Charisma comes from conviction—from WHY. If passion motivates, purpose inspires.

In any organization, WHY is typically represented by the CEO of the company; HOW by the senior executives, and WHAT by the employees. For every WHY-type, there is a HOW-type. Those who know WHY need those who know HOW. If WHY-types are visionary optimists, HOW-types are pragmatic realists. (Most people are HOW-types). Companies need both vision (WHY) and mission (HOW) statements. It's the difference between leading and running a company. Most companies have logos but not meaningful symbols. The former is about the company, the latter about the cause. We can put it this way in *four* points:

1. Attention—grab this from the outset

2. Interest—tell a story or anecdote

3. Desire—appeal to an implicit need

4. Action—make an explicit need easy (e.g., provide a contact email or provide a pay option for the product)

The Practice

Practice employing the above advice and ideas, or, at least, those aspects which resonate with you. In sum, pay attention in what you do to the following *seven*:

- Cultivate the five principles of rhetoric
- Deploy the three-step sequence of *ethos, pathos,* and *logos*
- Take into account Cicero's ten guidelines
- Consider joining toastmasters as well as listening to some great speeches
- Adopt some of Schopenhauer's thirty-eight tactics
- Draw on Dennett's seven rules for critical thinking
- Start with WHY

Milton Erickson's Hypnosis: Speech as Suggestion

Other tools have been utilized not only in business like Neuro-Linguistic Programming, but also by way of therapeutic interventions. One such is hypnosis, which has been integrated in advertising as much as in clinical psychotherapy. Especially worthy of mention are the insights into language patterns as evidenced in American psychiatrist Milton H. Erickson's (1901–1980) contributions to hypnotherapy.[2] Hypnosis attempts to induce a trance state in order to suggest and persuade a patient to a favorable outcome, for example, in regard to stopping smoking or losing weight. It operates by way of observation, utilization, and direction. Trance is a narrowing, focused state of attention, which makes patients more amenable to suggestions being communicated to the subconscious mind. Drugs, dance, lights, storytelling, chants etc. all can induce trance, which is heightened in hypnosis. The patient is then guided through visualization and imagery to optimal wellbeing. In a way, the process involves getting a person to daydream. Many of its detractors would argue that hypnotic suggestions rarely last and symptoms return. Moreover, it seems manipulative and a disingenuous short-circuiting of the subject's speech and conscious "working-through." Hypnotherapists say they are engaging in positive communication by way of mental rehearsal which aims at emotional, cognitive, and behavioral amelioration.

In terms of "persuasion," hypnosis might be compared to ancient rhetoric, one which operates on the subliminal level. One example of this is what is called the "agreement set," whereby a number of questions are asked which obtain an affirmative answer such as "Well, you found the address alright?," so the person is primed to answer accordingly with a "yes." He/she is then lead to more "yes" answers. Sometimes, a reverse set can be used but this still operates on the level of agreement. For example, "You're not going to want me to tell you anything you're not ready for?" Even here, when the answer is "no," there is still agreement. Truisms are frequently employed which are undeniable, such as "Lovely day out there," and these can be followed by "embedded suggestions." These can be compound or contingent, so they link things, for example, "you can hear my voice and you can relax." The hypnotherapist will pace, then lead ("As you listen to my voice, you begin to relax"). The language is presuppositional which directs the flow of conversation/communication to inevitabilities, which

---

2. See Erickson, *My Voice Will Go With You.*

presuppose positive expectations. The focus is on "when" things *will* happen rather than "whether" or if they will happen. Subtle semiotic sub-texts are deployed. The language will be "meaningfully vague" in that the hypnotherapist is eliciting information. Vague language is naturally hypnagogic. Binds are also utilized where the client is offered two or more choices, for example, "do you want to sit in this or that chair"? This implies they will sit in a chair! "I wonder whether you know you'll go into a trance?," is an example of a double bind. Clients can be intentionally confused by sentences such as, "You can forget to remember the things you forgot or remember to forget the things that you remember." Inside every indirect suggestion, according to Erickson, is a direct suggestion hiding. The aim is to bypass the conscious mind. Metaphors are also practiced within sessions, as well as anecdotes, allegories, and analogies. The emphasis is on the form not the changing contents—the pattern behind the problem. Finally, we can reference their **RIGAAR** model:

R: Rapport (establish a connection)

I: Information gathering (draw out the case-history)

G: Goal setting (set out the aims and objectives
    to be achieved/accomplished)

A: Accessing resources (discover what the client's
    strengths and skills are)

A: Agreeing a strategy (formulate an action-plan to move forward)

R: Rehearsal (picture things happening in the mind)

These principles have been enacted by stage-hypnotists as much as by salesmen in an attempt to subtly persuade, entice, and bait. There is also a whole other related debate concerning the placebo effect which stimulates healing, which is outside the remit of this discussion. We now move from rhetoric to dialectic in the following chapter.

"People generally quarrel because they cannot argue."—G. K. Chesterton

2

The Dialectic Method

SOCRATES (470/469–399 BC) WAS a philosopher who wrote nothing and who claimed to know nothing. What we know of him we mainly know through Plato's dialogues where he features (most of the time) as the main protagonist, as well as from students' reports (Xenophon and Aristophanes) He is an enigmatic figure who was executed by hemlock. He was informed by the Delphic oracle that there was none wiser than he. So, Socrates set out in his search for *sophia* (wisdom). He questioned many famous people around Athens who had a reputation for great erudition only to conclude that he was the wisest man because at least he knew that he didn't know anything. His father was a sculptor-stonemason and Socrates himself worked as one. His mother was a midwife. To some extent Socrates was a mental midwife—giving birth to ideas. His wife, Xanthippe, was of a quite different temperament, shall we say, to Socrates! Together, they had three sons. As youths were not allowed to enter the Agora (a central public space in ancient Greek city-states), they gathered in workshops surrounding it which Socrates frequented and where the famous conversations occurred.

His maieutic method (from the Greek meaning "to give birth") attempts, through a process of questioning and logical refutation (*elenchus*), to elicit truth. It's a form of cooperative "argumentative" dialogue between individuals which aims to stimulate thought by "drawing out" (the real meaning of "education') latent ideas and clarifying underlying assumptions.

Three Socratic Guidelines

1. Enter their world (*meet* your interlocutor where they are but don't *merge* with them).

2. Ask a two-legged question (honour the person's goals and aspirations while offering a new perspective). A Socratic question has two feet: one comes down in the interlocutor's/client's world, the second offers an additional perspective, unseen by the person. That's why maieutic questions tend to be surprising.

3. Offer only a few, carefully formulated questions (too many questions tend to confuse and control). Maieutic questions should be non-prying and non-prurient.

Examples of maieutic questions (especially for coaches or counsellors):

- As you look back on your life, what were the moments when you were most yourself?, happiest?

- What is a goal you would like to accomplish in one month? In six months?

- How do you find courage?, where do you find love, wonder, hope?

- What is a fear you would like to be free of?

- What challenge do you have before you right now?

- If you were asked by a child you love to tell the most important thing you have learned in life, what would it be?

- What is something you'd like to celebrate?

- What is life asking of you at this time, even in all your suffering?

- When do you feel most renewed and invigorated?

- What person do you most admire and why?

A Socratic Dialogue

A Socratic dialogue is a formal method by which a small group of people (circa 5–20), guided by a facilitator, finds an answer to a universal question, for example, "what is leadership?" or "what is love?" It can be any question on which the group decides. The aim: to discover what something is, to come up with a universal definition. The purpose is to reach the universal from the particular. It's group decision-making by consensus. There are no winners or losers. All the virtues of group-discussions prevail—patience, active listening, precise questions, attentiveness, civility, etc. Dialogues: can take place from two hours to two days.

A Socratic dialogue is not a hierarchical chain-of-command model. It's not a debate nor is it a committee meeting. It's a symphony not a solo endeavor. It's a co-operative search for a universal truth, which is discovered by all members of the group, analogous to a jury deliberation. Participants are bound by rules of rational discourse. Like a jury, the group will decide what evidence it weighs up. Socratic dialogues can be practiced in boardrooms and businesses, in creches and classrooms, on cruise ships and in conversational cafes (Socratic salons). There are *three* levels to a Socratic dialogue:

1. The discourse of the dialogue itself
2. The discourse about the direction of the dialogue
3. The (meta)discourse about the rules governing the dialogue

The facilitator of the Socratic dialogue is like the conductor of an orchestra. He has no voice in the score but has a meta-voice in conducting the performance. It has a specific shape, which may be likened to an hourglass. It is widest at the top and bottom, and narrowest at the waist. One begins at the top, with a universal question (e.g., what is leadership?).

Ten Rules of a Socratic Dialogue

1. Decide on the question (the group can do this in advance or on the day). Pose the question in the form of "what is . . . ?" "What is X?" works best. (If possible, select the question beforehand). For example: What is liberty?, what is leadership?, what is love?, what is happiness?, what is hope?

2. Each member of the group then reflects and is asked to give an example from his or her own life-experience that best illustrates/embodies X. It should be a first-hand account, closed in time, simple, and not too emotional. Everyone then briefly presents their examples to the group.

3. The group then chooses, by consensus, one of the examples as the focus of the dialogue to consider in depth.

4. The person who offered the example gives as detailed an account as possible, elaborating on it. Group members can question him/her for purposes of clarification.

5. The group must then decide exactly where in the example is the universal manifest. Where is the leadership, in this example? Thus, the group breaks down the whole story into its smallest component parts, asking "where did X occur?"

6. The group must then define X (e.g., leadership) in terms of a consensual articulation. The universal has thus been particularized. James Joyce: "the universal is contained within the particular."

7. The working definition is then re-applied to each of the other examples. So, here you return to the other personal experiences to see if they fit the definition. If the definition is truly universal it will fit/suit each example. If not, then:

8. It will need to be modified accordingly.

9. The group will then, at this final stage offer counterexamples, in an attempt to undermine or falsify or refine the definition.

10. The (universal) definition arrived at is articulated.

Group Guidelines

- Express doubts
- Be attentive to others
- Refrain from monologues
- Don't ask hypothetical questions
- Don't reference published works or quote
- Strive for consensus
- Should be a first-person experience
- Should be succinct, simple, and not too emotional
- Person in question should be willing to answer questions

Suggestion

Set up your own Socratic study-group or experiment. "Socratize" with someone—clarify their assumptions, helping to make them more objective. Contextualize your conversations (Socrates did this). E.g., with military leaders Socrates spoke about the virtue of courage; with an old school friend Lysis he debated the topic of friendship. Some examples of definitions include: "Love is to will the good of the other" (Plato); "Happiness is an activity of the soul in accordance with virtue" (Aristotle); "Evil is a lack of good" (Aquinas); "Hope is acting on an expectation for a preferred outcome consistent with one's current life-direction." (See the work of Leonard Nelson on Modern Socratic Dialogues [MSD] and one of my own books, *What is Friendship? Conversations with the Great Philosophers*).

Socratic Principles

We can distinguish *three* characteristics of Socrates's dialogues as written up by Plato: 1. There is only one answer—Socrates's interlocutors respond by saying "yes" a lot, or "it seems so"—they are persuaded by the truth; 2. Anyone can answer the questions; and 3. They are addressed to reason (which is common to all).

Listen

> "The purest form of listening is to listen without memory or desire."—
> Wilfred Bion

Absculta: "Listen" is the first word of the *Rule of St Benedict*. We need to practise active and *deep listening*—an auscultation of the heart. "Those who have ears to hear, let them hear." "Socrates teaches you how to listen" (Nietzsche).

> "Yes, I am a lover of your wisdom, my friend, and I am careful with it
> so that nothing you say will be lost."—Plato (*Euthyphro*)

Really *listen* to your conversation-partner. Pay attention to his words, to the sound of his voice. Listen with both ears. Listen to yourself listening to others. Conversation is speaking "with" not "at" another. Socrates never missed a single word spoken to him. Attentive listening brings us to the point of stillness—that condition which is needed for the operation of reason. In Sanskrit, the word for "hearing" is *shravanam*, which can be translated as "to hear" or "to listen," "to attend" or "be obedient to." The root is *shru* meaning "to wait upon" or "obey." Practise listening with interest and attention.

Questions for consideration

- How do you rate your ability to listen?

- How does listening affect the speaker, would you say?

- When you are listening to someone do you find yourself jumping ahead of them, pre-empting them or finishing their sentences for them?

- How often do you get irritated or impatient in a conversation, angry or defensive? In what situations?

- How often are you fully present to what's actually being said?

- Do you find your attention wandering? In what situations? What's capturing it?

Ask Open Questions

Open questions draw out, elicit information. Closed questions shut down conversation. There's a world of difference between: "do you drink?" and "when did you start drinking?" Each question leads on to other questions. Follow the thread. The key to asking good questions is presence of mind. Be clear. Socrates always enquires as to the *meaning* of things.

> "The reproach that is often made against me, that I ask questions of others and have not the wit to answer them myself, is very just."— Plato (*Theaetetus*)

> "But why, if I have a suspicion do I ask instead of telling you? Not for your sake, but in order that the argument may proceed in such a manner as is most likely to set forth the truth."—Plato (*Gorgias*)

Socrates wasn't interested in winning but on registering the truth of things.

Stick with a question until a conclusion appears

Don't wander off. Stick to the subject at hand. "Help me then to draw out the conclusion which follows from our admissions, for it is good to repeat and review what is good twice and thrice over, as they say" (Plato, *Gorgias*). Practice the *four* Rs of thoughts:

1. **Record** them
2. **Review** them
3. **Reflect** on them
4. **Respond** to them

Questions for consideration

- What stops you from going further with questions in a conversation or discussion?
- What subjects are off-limits? Why?
- What subjects do you have "firm ideas" about?
- Are you willing to be proved wrong?
- Do you stay on topic or find yourself introducing extraneous material?

Follow the truth

Let truth guide the discussion. The truth alone is persuasive. Socrates: " . . . it is necessary for the questioner to follow the answerer wherever the answerer may lead . . . " (Plato, *Euthyphro*). So, don't skip ahead. Try not to be formulating the next question. Wait until the other person has finished before formulating your answer. Stay with the unknown. Trust the process. Let the truth convince you, nothing else.

> "Do not be convinced by me Agathon. Be convinced by the truth."—Plato (*Symposium*)

> "It has been my fixed principle to speak the truth."—Plato (*Apology*)

Suggestions

- Think of yourself as a thinker.
- Take your time.
- Don't personalise.
- Try not to get *reactive*; rather, *respond* with reason.
- Ask specific questions that focus directly on the subject under consideration.
- Always respect your interlocutor—there is no such thing as a stupid question.
- Create a questioning climate in your home/workplace.
- Practice active listening; pay attention to the speaker and to the said.

So:

- Pause—take time out to reflect and think and question
- Ponder—generate ideas and insights and innovations
- Pose questions—deconstruct the dominant paradigm; challenge convention
- Produce something meaningful
- Proceed—pave the way ahead

"When one is freed and gets on his feet and turns his head and walks towards the light—all he has seen till now was false and a trick, but now he sees more truly."—Plato (*Republic*)

The Giraffe Exercise

Socrates stuck his neck out. When did you take a stance on something? When did you stick your neck out to speak an uncomfortable truth to someone? Who would you say are the Socratic gadflies of our time?

Friendship and Fine Conversation

Enjoy good conversations in good company (*Satsanga*: a Sanskrit word meaning "to associate" or "be in the company of true people").

> "When a group of friends have enjoyed fine conversation together, you will find that suddenly something extraordinary happens. As they are speaking, it's as if a spark ignites, passing from one speaker to another, and as it travels, it gathers strength, building into a warm and illuminating flame of mutual understanding which none of them could have achieved alone."—Plato (*Critias*)

Alcibiades said about Socrates: "He seems to see into my soul."

Question for consideration

- What do you value most in your conversations?
  What makes them meaningful?
- Think of the best *three* conversations you've ever had.
  What made them so great?

In Plato's dialogue, *Laches*, which has courage as its subject matter, defined as wise endurance of the soul, Socrates says philosophy should be practical and engage in "the care of the soul." True conversation/communication should create harmony between the speaker and his words. He describes such a "man" as "musical." They produce "the most beautiful harmony" not on a lyre or flute but by "rendering his own life harmonious by fitting his deeds to his words." One could say that this is the preeminent Socratic proposition: we must match our actions with our speech, and be sincere.

Walk the talk and say what you mean

Plato's dialogue, *Gorgias*, is all about communication/conversation. Gorgias was a famous teacher of oratory; he was loosely considered a Sophist. Socrates (through Plato) makes it clear from the offset where he is coming from when he describes Gorgias as a teacher of rhetoric (public speaking) but not of virtue! Gorgias has skills of persuasion. Socrates traps him in a contradiction, forcing him to admit that a skilled orator must actually *know* something about the subject on which he is speaking so persuasively!

Polus seems overwhelmed by the thought that rhetoric gives a person the power to do exactly as one pleases, even injustice, if that suits the situation. Against Polus, Socrates says it is better to suffer injustice than to do it. Callicles likewise admires the life of pleasure and power, while Socrates champions the philosophical life of wisdom and virtue, committing himself to the objective existence of justice, devoting himself (he was 71 when he died) to what we might nowadays call "lifelong learning" (for its own sake).

Devote yourself to the ongoing, self-motivated pursuit of knowledge for personal and/or professional development

Socrates will insist that we always examine/explore our beliefs, presumptions, and presuppositions; exposing them to the light of true reason. We might call this an "Examen of Consciousness," to employ St. Ignatius's term who, in his *Spiritual Exercises*, put forward what he called the "Presupposition": Always presuppose that your interlocutor is more ready to put a good interpretation on your statements rather than to condemn them as false and if your conversation partner really doesn't understand you, correct him with kindness, using appropriate means to bring him to a correct interpretation, so as to defend the proposition from error. Like Socrates, Ignatius will insist that we *question ourselves*.

In the *Gorgias*, Socrates paints a pretty negative picture of the practice of rhetoric; in the *Phaedrus*, he finds legitimate use for it, so long as it is kept subordinate to philosophy. Rhetoric does not convey the truth, according to Socrates—the truth is known only through philosophical study. By contrast, the speech of rhetoricians is motivated by the desire to win. We may advise thus: **Study (spend some time reading) philosophy.**

Socrates informs Polus who had said that rhetoric was "the most admirable of all the crafts" that he (Polus) had devoted himself to *oratory* rather than *discussion*. So, we might summarise the differences between rhetoric and dialectic thus:

Rhetoric—form of flattery—winning (persuasion): power

vs

Dialectic—logical discussion—wisdom (philosophy): truth

Socrates expounds the following central principle: "Be willing to give a brief answer to what you're asked" and to be wise in what you're speaking about. Socrates: "Curb your long style of speech."

Keep your speech short and base it on things you have knowledge of

When asked by Socrates what is it that oratory is, Gorgias retorts that it is the greatest good—the ability to persuade others by your speeches in lawcourts is wonderful because you make them your slave. Socrates sums it up thus: "oratory is a producer of persuasion." He wants to show Gorgias and the others that there is true and false knowledge, that "oratory produces the persuasion that comes from being convinced, and not the persuasion that comes from teaching, concerning what's just and unjust." So, rhetoric is shallow—all show, and no substance. The rhetorician "should use oratory justly."

Speak what is excellent (the true) and not what is expedient (the useful)

Socrates maintains that he doesn't want to win one over on his interlocutor. Moreover, one should be *pleased* to be refuted if what one says is untrue (false knowledge). "If you refute me, I shan't be upset but regard you as my greatest benefactor." So:

Always be willing to be proven wrong

Socrates's problem with oratory is that it "doesn't need to have any knowledge of the state of their subject matters; it only needs to have discovered some device to produce persuasion in order to make itself appear to those who don't have knowledge that it knows more than those who actually do have it." An orator should never want to do anything unjust. Of course, when spoken to, Socrates reminds us that we do have the freedom to leave, so give yourself permission to do so if you believe it's getting nowhere or becoming fractious.

You can walk away from an argument, you know

Socrates goes on to tell Polus that he doesn't think rhetoric is a craft at all! Rather, it's a "knack," for "producing a certain gratification and pleasure." There's nothing serious or admirable about it. He places it with cosmetics and sophistry, saying it's something shameful. "I call it flattery." It's basically fraudulent. It takes no thought at all of whatever is best. It pretends, perpetrates, and perpetuates deception. Polus opines that orators have the greatest power in and over the city. Socrates couldn't disagree more, asserting that they have the least power. (Because power can be seen as doing what one sees fit without intelligence). It brings to mind Lord Acton's famous saying: power corrupts, and absolute power corrupts absolutely. *Power opposes truth.* That's why Plato always insists on temperance, justice, and wisdom and not just courage, on the *unity* of the virtues. For Socrates, doing what's unjust is the worst thing there is. "I would choose suffering over doing what's unjust." We may formulate this principle in the following way:

Always put your speech in the service of what is good/right/just

The happy person is the just person, is the good person. The wicked are truly miserable. Socrates: "What's true is never refuted." Poverty, disease, and injustice are three states of corruption. By contrast, "The happiest man, then, is the one who doesn't have any badness in his soul." Strive to be a good person and you will be happy as a consequence/side-effect.

Guard against injustice. As oratory can be used to defend injustice, rhetoric must be engaged in cautiously, to say the least. Philosophy is less fickle than flattery. "What philosophy says always stays the same." Philosophy is not a crowd pleaser like rhetoric; it's about being in harmony with oneself (self-mastery, rather than mastering others). Socrates quotes Euripides: "allotting the greatest part of the day to this [philosophy], where he finds himself at his best." Polus is not persuaded, even going on to assert that to practise philosophy when you're older is "ridiculous" and that such a person needs a good flogging! Socrates prefers a soul made of gold, full of knowledge, good-will and frankness. Socrates commends philosophy to us as a way of life dedicated to temperance (self-control) and ruling the pleasures and passions within oneself. "Nothing to excess" was the second Delphic dictum, after "Know yourself." To know yourself one must know true measure. Such is the middle path of moderation. Those who have attained such inner order/organization are happier than those "disordered" souls, for the former are in tune/touch with themselves—aligned, in sync with their souls and their divine nature.

Discussion aims at mutual exploration

Socrates next distinguishes pleasure from happiness because "there is some pleasure that isn't good." The Good can't be reduced to just unrestricted enjoyment. "For pleasant and painful things come to a stop simultaneously, whereas good things and bad ones do not because they are in fact different things." Pleasure aims at mere gratification rather than the good. Hence Socrates enquires of Callicles if orators always speak with regard to what's best. "Do they always set their sights on making the citizens as good as possible through their speeches?" or are they solely bent on plamausing the crowd (and themselves)? *The pleasant is to be done for the sake of the good.* The good in an inner excellence; it has a certain order in the soul (*psyche*), as well as in the state (*polis*). Indeed, there is a world order, a uni-verse (one song), which is a *cosmos* (ordered whole) rather than a chaos of conflict and confusion.

Conversation should aim at wisdom rather than winning or point-scoring

To philosophize in this Socratic and Platonic sense is to learn how to dialogue, and how to die. One should "not be attached to life." The aim is to make the soul (self) as good as possible—this alone is noble. And to care for the city and its citizens—to be concerned for truth. Callicles: "Do you want me to agree with you?" Socrates: "Yes, if you think that what I say is true." This is what differentiates a leader (who leads himself first then the citizens to truth) from the orator who is really the one and the same as the sophist. Actually (more Socratic irony), sophistry is to be more admired than oratory. Leaders are ready *to serve* rather than *to flatter*, which is the function of rhetoric, i.e., to say what you think other people want to hear. Socrates: "So I disregard the things held in honour by the majority of people, and by practising truth I really try, to the best of my ability, to be and to live as a very good man, and when I die, to die like that. And I call on all other people as well . . . . to this way of life." This is worth all contests and debates.

Don't just say what you think people want to hear, rather, speak the truth

Ask open-ended rather than closed questions. Socrates says the speeches he makes do not aim at gratification "but at what's best." Say or do nothing unjust to either man or gods. Socrates exclaims that if he came to his end because of a deficiency in "flattering oratory," he'd bear his death with ease and equanimity (as indeed he did). The Platonic point is to depart life with one's soul in order and not stuffed full of unjust actions. Such a person when he dies, departs for the Isles of the Blessed "to make his abode in complete happiness, beyond the reach of evils." Those who have lived unjustly go to "the prison of payment and retribution, the one they call Tartarus." So: Be your best rather than base self.

> "My way toward the truth is to ask the right questions."—
> Plato (*Protagoras*)

Socrates always takes his lead from the other person, actively listening and following the thread of the discourse. He never personalises and accords his conversation partner respect. He *responds* (with reason) rather than *reacts* (with passion). In a dialectical discussion, both parties are changed by the experience. Above all, Socrates embodies *presence*—he is really there; he meets the person when they are (context) rather than when they're not—he strives to understand their particular viewpoint. He appeals always to *experience* and gives countless *examples* of what he means.

Assume your interlocutor might just know something that you don't

What survives refutation is this: doing what's unjust is more to be guarded against than suffering injustice. It's about *being* good and not just *seeming* to be good that counts. Indeed, that's what we need to take care of more than anything else. So, every form of flattery, Socrates contends and concludes, should be avoided. Oratory (and every other activity) is always to be in support of what's just and true and good. Socrates: "Listen to me; follow me to where I am." And you will be happy during life and at its end, even if people demean you or throw dirt at you. You will remain unaffected if you are "an admirable and good man who practices excellence." The best way of life is philosophy whose golden aim is "to practice justice and the rest of excellence both in life and in death" and not rhetoric whose aim is "to sound off as through we're somebodies." The Platonic objective is ultimately this existentially exalted one: to *create joy in the soul and justice in society.*

True Communication

Real communication is a *communion*—the marriage of two minds which has, as its primary purpose, the discovery of truth through words. *E pluribus unum*: "out of many, one." True communication, which derives from the Latin *communicare* meaning "to share," takes place when the speaker and listener become one and there is this profound unity. Its secondary job, as it were, is the exchange of information. Similarly, *con-versation* is the process of "together-versing" (flowing together)—the very opposite of *contro-versy*, which is the process of "contra-versing" (flowing against). Conversation is a work of synthesis. True conversation has this underlying principle from the Gospels: "Where two or three are gathered in my name, there am I in the midst of them" (*Matthew* xviii, 20). All true conversation calls upon the transcendent Centre.

But speech is not the only means of communication. There is writing, silence, our gestures. Even the clothes we wear and the cars we drive tells a story about us. There is covert (subtle) communication where no sounds are needed, such as between two lovers. Society communicates through its literature and laws, architecture, and art. However, speech is the most powerful means of communication. *Two* rules given by the wise, which sum up the essence of *loving speech*:

1. Never speak an unpleasant truth (speak the truth pleasantly, in other words)

2. Never tell a pleasant lie

Language gives being. Language is the house of being. We should care for the Word. When someone speaks, he needs an Other to listen. We need to hearken to the words of the Other. "Obedience" in Latin means "listening to." "Having ears, they hear not."

According to Martin Heidegger, the 20th century German philosopher, we can use language as **assertion** (logical propositions), which serves the threefold aim of a) designating (this thing here); b) predicating (this thing here is white); and c) communicating (the exchange of such designated and predicated information); or as **interpretive discourse** (hermeneutics) which sees things as signs and symbols to be decoded and deciphered. Here, discourse can be **authentic** or **inauthentic**. Authentic communication Heidegger calls *Saying* (this requires our ability to fall silent so as to listen and genuinely respond to the voice of Being and be responsible for our speech). The privileged paradigm here is poetic language which "deworlds" me—it takes me out of myself and introduces something alien so that the familiar and foreign fuse. Words operate by way of uncanny dispossession. This way of communicating takes us out of the pragmatic world of consumption and production so that, to take an example, a rose is not just a horticultural object to be watered or plucked; nor an emblem of national identity (the Rose of England); or of sexual purity or resurrection (the risen Rose); but in poetic utterance, the rose exceeds, surpasses, all our existential interpretations and is allowed *to be itself*. Thus, the rose exists *without why*, as an extra in existence. Inauthentic communication, by contrast, is empty cocktail-party conversation. It is idle chatter, public opinion, gossip, the language of "the They" (crowd). It is anonymous chit chat, prattle, babble. If authentic communication is Real speech, inauthentic discourse is Empty speech—mere verbiage; double-speak. The Shankaracharya in a conversation once said, "So much use is made of the word "these days" but nothing seems to mean anything." This is aptly described by Yeats in his poem, *Easter 1916*, as "polite meaningless words." One is not defiled by what goes into one's mouth (meat, for example) but by what comes out of one's mouth (our words). The way we speak affects our being and that of others. Speaking words that do not agitate, that are loving, beneficial, and true preserves one's being in truth. We may describe this as the lawful way to speak, by which I mean, living and speaking in harmony with the eternal law. Others include patience, taking from life only what you need, etc.

> "Obedient to the voice of being, thought seeks the word through which the truth of Being may be expressed."—Martin Heidegger

So, idle chat is not true communication, nor is not saying what you mean (duplicity/deceitfulness), nor lying, criticism, hyperbolic speech, manipulative speech, frozen silence, heavy sighs etc. We must be on perpetual guard against these forms of empty speech. True (authentic) communication is always in pursuit of truth and wisdom. You must always say what you mean (match your words with your thoughts). Repetition and exaggerated speech reduce the power of speech. Truth is terse and exists *now*. True speech never causes pain. The advice from the wise is never speak a pleasant untruth or an unpleasant truth. Learn to speak the truth pleasantly. Have no company with untruth.

Ask yourself: who is speaking here? Is it the ego or the true Self? Who are my words in service to? My ego seeks to protect and preserve its image through persuasion, lies (see my book *The Truth about Lying*) or violence/force. The Self wishes only for truth. Ego-centric speech attempts to destroy the other's arguments without any real communication occurring through put downs, sarcasm, belittling, denouncing etc. Egoic speech doesn't listen; it simply wants you to agree with it, to convert you to its viewpoint on every subject. On the other hand, the speech emanating from the Self is truth-centred; it enquires openly, possessing no fixed view, interested always in the Other and grateful when proved wrong.

The effects of ego-centric speech are the following: you cling to error even when you know you're wrong; you claim to know what you do not know; you justify yourself; you take a stance on a subject; you find yourself developing a whole plethora of conflicting voices; and you don't really say what needs to be said, only what you think the Other wants to hear. The ego closes down communication. The ego speaks *at* someone rather than *to* someone.

There are different styles of speech. Some may be emotional, others factual, some sparse with their words, others effluent. This can give rise to miscommunications. Some people may not have the words at their disposal to say what they are thinking or feeling. The key is to listen from the heart and talk from the head. Drop egoic, empty speech. Practise true communication, from Self to Self. Listen to the sound of your own voice—after all, you want others to listen to you! When you're having a conversation, remain open to both sides in the debate. Speak naturally (be your Self). Don't rehearse what you have to say if possible or parrot the discourse of an Other. There are only ever two activities occurring in conversation: speaking and listening. So, when someone else is speaking, really listen—stay with the speaker not just with his words. Meet the person where he is, not where he's not, as Socrates did. Practise what you preach. Don't speak to someone who isn't listening/paying attention. It is so much wasted breath. Just stop speaking! Above all, conserve speech. Let your words be economical, efficient. Avoid talking for the sake of talking. Have something to say. Deliver a speech in love (with integrity and conviction). Conversation, if it is to be real, connects people especially through eye-contact. So, be present and pay attention. Separate the person from the event (don't personalise through invective or spite). Speech should convey knowledge and love—truth and reason.

Avoid internal talk. Cultivate interior silence. The deepest form of communication is when you converse with yourself in the silence and stillness of meditation. All our words end ultimately with the Great Silence. This is the silence, not of resignation, but of reverence before the All/ Whole/Mystery.

Styles of Speech

Every person has their own inimitable style of speech. Speeches can move us for good or ill. One can distinguish *three* types of speech. Barack Obama, for example, uses speech to unify and reconcile. His speeches are inclusive; he asks for sacrifice and service. Obama speaks to the *head*. Dr Martin Luther King's speeches are emotional; he appeals to the *heart*. Hitler's speeches come from the *gut*; they are orders to action. All speeches are either based on rhetoric/persuasion (becoming) or dialectic/reason (being). The former sells something and is based on opinion, while the latter offers certainty and is based on universal reason/truth. Indeed, most speech is rhetoric. But there is one other type of speech and that's internal speech—the silent speech in the head which tells us stories such as "I'm afraid of spiders." This speech we need to change because it comes from the past and is mostly untrue. Thoughts are a form of speech. We have been telling ourselves stories (thoughts in our head) for years. Indeed, creation itself comes about via speech ("In the beginning was the Word"). Speech, so, is the first act of consciousness. Creation is sustained in sound. Hence, the importance of a mantra (or sound-based repetition) in meditation which stills the mind. Indeed, the (Eastern) symbol of "A-U-M" which forms a Trinity, comes out as "OM" (the movement from /A/ to /U/ becomes /O/). These three sounds are really one (just like the three divine persons are one, in other words, three aspects of one consciousness). You can hear this same sound in a baby's "Mama." When we go beyond speech to its source, we encounter the silent Ground of being. Hence the injunction to "be still and know that I am God." This involves going backstage where it is silent and in silence, we find ourselves. The Self is beyond speech. Real thinking is silent.

True Dialogue

Dialogue is a dynamic process of meaning-making. The term stems from the Greek for conversation: *dialogos*, consisting of *Dia* ("through") and *Logos* ("reason" or "speech"). The first person to deploy the term was Plato, whose work is chiefly concerned with the art of dialectic. Most of Plato's writings are in the form of dialogues featuring Socrates converse on various philosophical topics with his interlocutors. Other philosophers who have employed the genre include Malebranche, Berkeley, Hume, Santayana, Stein, Iris Murdoch, and Viktor Frankl (see his play). Martin Buber assigns dialogue a pivotal role in his theology/philosophy (see his *I and Thou*). For Buber, dialogue is an existential encounter, a meeting, the very prerequisite of authentic relationship "between man and man" and man and God. True dialogue is characterised by openness, honesty, and mutual commitment. We are led from individual monologue to personal dialogue. Paulo Freire advanced dialogue as a tool and type of pedagogy for the oppressed, as a praxis for liberation.

"Judge a man by his questions rather than his answers."—Voltaire

"The wise man doesn't give the right answers; he poses the right questions."—Claude Levi-Strauss

Answer the question. Question the answer. Ask good questions. This is what I heard recently on a Dublin tram:

"Mummy?"

"Yes darling?"

"Why are we going so slow?"

"Because the tram is long."

"Why are we going so slow?"

"Because we're going around the corner."

"Mummy, why are we going so slow?"

"Because we have to stop at the next stop to let people on."

"Mummy, why are we going so slow?"

"Oh, look at all the people waiting to get on."

Momentary silence.

"Mummy, why are we still going so slow?"

It is estimated that mothers are asked more questions in an hour than a teacher or doctor. Questioning organizes thinking around what we don't know. Curiosity indicates aliveness. **ASK: Always Seek Knowledge.** Knowledge yes, but knowledge of what? Reality, of course, and of ourselves.

Knowledge is having the right answers; intelligence is asking the right questions. Einstein once remarked, "It's not that I am so smart, but I stay with the questions much longer." The poet Maria Rainer Rilke enjoins us to stay with the questions, to linger a while with them, and to live them.

"Live the questions now."—Maria Rainer Rilke

Life is about asking questions, about asking ourselves questions, such as "Who am I?," "What is it all about?," "What is the point and purpose of existence?" "What ought I do?" Life confronts us with questions, interrogates us. It is life that places questions before us. It is a call to listen then respond. It's a Q&A session.

We are compelled to question, impelled, propelled into so doing. It's as if we are thrown onto the stage with no script; we don't know our lines or our exits and entrances. We don't even know what the play is about. About this play the German philosopher Immanuel Kant wanted answers to *four* fundamental questions: What can I know? What ought I do? What does it mean to be? For what may I hope?

My hope, dear reader, is that you will tarry a while with the interrogative because the answers you get depend on the questions you ask. You will soon see that in truth there is really only one question—The Question, which is a quest into the heart of your own being. We might call this "the self-appropriation of interiority" (Self-attention), which is something about knowing who you are in truth.

"The riddle does not exist. If a question can be put at all, then it can also be answered."—Ludwig Wittgenstein

"The important thing is not to stop questioning; curiosity
has its own reason for existing."—Albert Einstein

In his *The Myth of Sisyphus,* Albert Camus, the French philosopher, famously announced that there was only one truly philosophical question and that is "should we commit suicide?" It was Shakespeare's too: "To be or not to be? That is the question." Taking a lead from Leibnitz, Heidegger enquired, "why is there something rather than nothing?," while Friedrich Nietzsche, for his part, felt that "why has no answer." Traditionally, *five* questions have been offered:

Whys Up

The Five Ws:

1. What?
2. Who?
3. When?
4. Where?
5. Why?

They just about sum it all up—our all too human quest-ioning, our demand for clarity, our existential exigency for meaning and for answers in the face of "the unreasonable silence of the world" (Camus).

To take *three* questions, as an example: what?, how? and why?. *What* you are doing is your *work, how* you are doing it is your *attitude* toward your work and *why* you are doing it is the *purpose* around it. Asking questions makes us whyser/wiser. The philosopher who made a career from asking questions was Socrates. He prodded and probed. He was a gadfly. His questions stung his contemporary Athenians into an awareness of their ignorance, into what they didn't know, but should have known. Ultimately, he was put to death for his questions. There is a story (legend) told about Socrates (another legend!) and his Triple Filters' Test.

The Test of Three

Pass the Threefold Test. One can set this out in a Socratic or Sufi version. Let's Socratize it first. One day Socrates, who was widely lauded for his wisdom, came upon an acquaintance who ran up to him excitedly and said, "Socrates, do you know what I just heard about one of your students?"

"Wait a moment," Socrates replied. "Before you tell me, I'd like to pass it through a little test. It's called the Test of Three."

"Test of Three?"

"That's correct," Socrates continued. "Before you talk to me about my student, let's take a moment to test what you're going to say." He paused.

"The first test is Truth. Have you made absolutely sure that what you are about to tell me is true."

"No," the man replied, "actually, I just heard about it."

"All right," said Socrates. "So, you don't really know if it's true or not. Now let's try the second test, the test of Goodness. Is what you are about to tell me about my student something good?"

"No, on the contrary . . . ."

"So," Socrates continued, "you want to tell me something bad about him even though you're not certain it's true?"

The man shrugged, a little embarrassed.

Socrates continued: "You may still pass with the third test—the filter of Utility. Is what you want to tell me about my student going to be useful to me?"

"No, not really . . . ."

"Well," concluded Socrates, "if what you want to tell me is neither true nor good nor even useful, why tell it to me at all?"

The man was defeated and ashamed and said no more.

The spiritual writer Eknath Easwaran (1910–1999) suggested that the Sufis advised us to speak only after our words managed to pass through three gates. At the first gate we ask ourselves: "Are these words true?" At the second gate we ask: "Are they necessary?" At the last gate we ask: "Are they kind?"

The Art of Conversation: Three Tips

A conversation is an interactive communication between two or more people. Conversation can cover polite discourse, small talk, banter, chats etc. When you engage in conversation, apply this Socratic scrutiny, and ask yourself:

1. Is it true?

2. Is it good?

3. Is it useful?

The Conversation, circa 1935, by Arnold Borisovich Lakhovsky. Source: Wiki Commons.

Communication derives from the Latin *communicare* meaning "to share." It's the art of conveying meanings through signs, symbols, signifiers and semiotic rules. There is verbal and non-verbal communication. Barriers to effective communication include filtering, selection perception, information overloads, emotions, language, silence, conversation apprehension, gender differences, political correctness, ambiguity in speech, the use of complex words or jargon. The hope is that good communication leads to better understanding. Contemporary commentators have put forward a checklist for effective communication. These are the seven Cs of communication:

The 7 Cs of Communication

Source: The World of Work. https://worldofwork.io/2019/07/
the-7-cs-of-communication/.

Be:

1. *Clear*: The message should possess clarity and be easily comprehensible to the recipient.

2. *Correct*: The message should be devoid of grammatical and spelling mistakes; it should be exact.

3. *Complete*: The message should be comprehensive and include all the relevant information required by the intended audience.

4. *Concrete*: The message should be specific with no room for misinterpretation; facts and figures should be given.

5. *Concise*: The message should be precise and to the point. Lengthy sentences should be avoided. Be short and snappy, conveying the subject matter in the least possible words.

6. *Considerate*: Be contextual. Take account of the receiver's opinions, knowledge, mindset, background, etc.

7. *Courteous*: Take into account the feelings and viewpoint of the receiver; show respect.

A Socratic dialogue is a spiritual exercise and a little like dying in that we are bid to let go of some of our own most cherished opinions and presuppositions as our conversation-partners challenge and change our conceptions;

it's a mutually enhancing process of enrichment. It's an *askesis* or discipline of desire, whose principal aim is self-transformation, one wrought through compassion rather than combat. At best it's a contemplative existential exercise, the point of which is to achieve or arrive at a certain self-transcendence. In examining our beliefs, we come to know ourselves better.

The Practice

Below are *twenty* Socratic suggestions for a good discussion:

- Really listen
- Be present
- Meet the person where they are without merging with them
- Ask open questions
- Don't personalize
- Take the conversational context into account
- Stick with the question
- Let yourself be led by the truth
- Say what you mean
- Pursue knowledge
- Aim for mutual understanding/exploration
- Keep your speech short
- Be willing to be refuted

> "Those who never retract their opinions love themselves
> more than they love the truth."—Joseph Joubert

- Put your speech in the service of the excellent rather than the expedient
- Strive for wisdom rather than winning
- Be authentic rather than a crowd-pleaser
- Assume your interlocutor can teach you something
- Engage with "full" rather than "empty" speech
- Ensure your speech passes the triple test
- Remember the 7 Cs of communication

"Wise men speak because they have something to say; Fools because they have to say something."—Plato

Public Speaking

Let's briefly provide some tips on public speaking. You may want to:

a. Persuade

b. Inform

c. Entertain

So, firstly determine your **goal**. What is the point and purpose of your speech? Secondly, determine its **duration**—how long your speech is going to be. Ideally, a speech should never be longer than 40 minutes, which is the average attention span of an adult. (Incidentally, Martin Luther King's "I have a dream" speech lasted 17 minutes). Find out who your **target** audience is—what type of people? Consider the amount of people present, their ages, interests, backgrounds etc. What are their **expectations**—these need to be taken into account. In any speech, pre-empt objections, give examples and generally be empathetic.

Next, you need to consider the kind of **language** you're going to use. Will it be formal or informal, light-hearted, or serious? Strive to be simple, clear and connect. Remind yourself what you need for your speech by way of **equipment**, such as laptop, leads, USB sticks, projector etc. Preferably, visit the location beforehand and test the technology. In terms of the speech itself, figure out what you want to say—your **main points** and how to *develop* them. Think of the **topics** you will highlight and the **transitions** you will make between key sentences. What are the **facts** that support your key points? It's not only about *what* you want to say but *how* you want to say it. Are you going to tell a story or joke? In terms of **pattern**, will you be chronological, spatial, analytical? In relation to content, will you be introducing metaphor, lists, catchphrases (e.g., Obama's "Yes we can"), irony, twists? Explore what **figures of speech** you might deploy.

The *"dispositio"* is the *structure* of your speech. Begin with a **hook** that grabs/catches the audience's attention—something by way of *intrigue*. It could be a story or soundbite or quote. Introduce yourself—say who you are to establish **credibility**. Ask yourself about your speech's *relevance*— why should anyone be interested? The main part should address a:

> **promise**—what they will get
>
> **problem**—which you're going to solve or shed light on, and
>
> **solution**—how you will satisfy the needs of your audience

Conclude with a **recap** (summary), a **call to action** and a **benefit** (reasons for). The *dénouement* is the appropriate time for a peroration—dramatic climax.

After writing your speech out in a *draft* form first, concentrate on *acting* the speech. After all, delivery is a performance. Think about your **tone**, **volume**, and **rhythm** in terms of low, medium, or high, as well as **gestures**. Below are *five* types of speeches:

1. *Antonius*: strongly motivational, voice of persuasion, used at the end of a speech usually.

2. *Cato*: voice of authority—to show leadership.

3. *Crassus*: voice of laughter and jokes.

4. *Demosthenes*: voice of calmness such as you find with gurus or therapists.

5. *Scipio*: voice of anger and indignation.

> "The single biggest problem with communication is the illusion that it has taken place."—George Bernard Shaw

Meta-Messages

Communication can operate on several different planes. For example, Jack says to Joan: "You're an idiot," then adds, "Just joking." Jack has sent two messages to Joan. The second message is about the first message. The second message told Joan that the first message wasn't meant to be taken seriously. Messages such as this second one, which are about other messages, are called "meta-messages." They operate on a different plane—a "meta-plane." And we're familiar with them. Body-language acts as body meta-language. It acts as a message about our verbal messages.

If Jack says to Joan, "You're an idiot," but is smiling, then his tone of voice and bodily gestures serve as meta-messages telling Joan that he is just joking. On the other hand, if Jack is tense and flushed and shouts,

"You're an idiot," then it is obvious to Joan that he's furious with her. In both cases the verbal message was the same ("You're an idiot") but the meta-message altered the meaning substantially, which suggests that for us to understand we must accurately identify its context by assigning an appropriate meta-message to it.

Four Levels of Speech

We have all heard the expression "freedom of speech," but how free are we when we speak? Do we speak from a place of constriction and restriction within ourselves—from a place of interference or real, expansive freedom? Vedic philosophy postulates *four* levels of speech:

Name	Location
Vaikhari	Tongue
Madhyama	Larynx
Pashyanti	Heart
Para	Navel

All speech has its origins in *para*—this is pure consciousness. Speech starts in the navel, where there is no movement or vibration. It passes through all levels. *Pashyanti* is speech centered on the heart—this is a poised state, full of potential, a still state. *Madhyama* is where sound reaches—this is when we are aware of it. We can hear it in the mind (mental realm) before it is spoken out loud. *Vaikhari* is when the word is spoken—it is the stage when speech manifests itself in physical form. So, we're aware of speech before it's spoken—in emotional or mental realms or in complete stillness. With wisdom, there is full connection with all four levels and complete freedom of speech. In ignorance, there is no such freedom.

We say, "it just tripped off my tongue" or "we had a good heart to heart" or "I've a good mind to tell him." Speech that is cut off from these deeper levels is superficial, shallow. At the *vaikhari* level, speech is glib. Speech at the *madhyama* level carries conviction. Here we say what we really think or believe or feel. It all depends on our level of connection. Fear or confusion can stop the person from really speaking, can hamper and hinder true communication. So, a good practice to develop is to become aware of what level of speech it is from which we're talking and listen, not only to how the other is speaking, but to how you're speaking. Many arguments occur when we personalize our conversations. *Para* is impersonal and therefore a source of great freedom as well as truth.

Incorporating the above, Adi Shankara, the eighth-century Indian philosopher who consolidated the doctrine of Advaita Vedanta, distinguished *three* forms of discussion.

Three Forms of Discussion

1. The aim here is to arrive at truth (akin to Socratic dialectic). Personal matters are secondary.

2. The aim here is to want to express your opinion—to have them prevail.

3. Here the aim is to carp—it's being critical and querulous, niggling, caviling (making petty and unnecessary objections).

In the first form, we conduct the conversation philosophically rather than personally. This level gives most freedom and is the best form of dialogue. In the second form, there tends to be a drive present and the discussion becomes overheated, as each participant is intent on presenting their opinions on the subject, to have their say no matter what. In the third type of discussion, the aim is to undermine, to highjack the conversation, to deride or scupper it. Truth is replaced by belligerence.

We need to try to respond rather than react, to rest and stop browbeating our "opponent" with the "truth" of our perspectives, to go quieter, to locate that still center within us—then we will move from deadlock into dialogue. Sometimes we've to surrender our convictions to the silence and simply rest, to let go of the emotional component which has taken hold. Dialectic happens in dialogue when we become free from false preconceptions, presuppositions, and prejudices. Socrates never missed a word of what his interlocutors were saying—he picked up on their attitudes and assumptions. A real dialogue is a spiritual exercise (*askēsis*), a good starting-point of which is the *epoché* or bracketing (suspension) of our natural way of thinking and speaking. Just park what we think, for the duration of the dialogue. Maybe we're mistaken—about a whole lot of things. Perhaps we might learn something new here or understand ourselves better. Isn't this a better motivation than merely sounding off, than speaking for the sake of speaking? After all, mere words we can get from anybody. Poets and prophets don't waste words—they have something to say. They lay bare the truth of things. Storytellers see into the still, sad music of humanity.

3

Stories and Symbols

"The story will save us."—Plato

Stories

WE COMMUNICATE, CONVINCE, AND connect with each other through stories. Stories are more compelling than facts. We are storytellers by nature. Telling stories seems basic to human beings. Stories help us make sense of that which is. Hesiod tells us how the founding myths (*mythos* = story) were invented to explain how the world came into existence. Aristotle was the first philosopher to set out a theory of storytelling in his *Poetics*, where he defined myth as *mimesis*—dramatic imitation and the plotting of human action. We can set out a *five*-step sequence in a story.

A Five-Step Sequence

1. Plot—what it is about (essence, formal cause of the story). Plots are concrete particulars, loose threads on the tapestry. For some, life is a masterpiece (a divine design); for others, it's a mess (chaotic) or a misery.

2. Setting—time. The past is looked upon by a *present* consciousness; the future is looked forward to by a *present* consciousness. We can contrast *Kronos* or material time (possibly "a tale told by an idiot, full of sound and fury, signifying nothing") with *Kairos* or spiritual

time—we are part of the painting of history, the never-ending story. (Whatever has been realized has been eternalized).

3. The Characters—presence of real or invisible people (*esse est co-esse*: to be is to be-with). For Martin Buber, "All living is a meeting." Examples are the Ego: player performing its part; the Self: directing the show. And who might the author of the play be? The cast of characters: apes, angels, dogs, and gods etc.

4. The Theme—what is the moral of the story, the meaning of life? The traditional answer from Aristotle to Freud has been happiness or objective flourishing for Aristotle (more like joy), and subjective satisfaction for Freud (more like pleasure). Neither pleasure nor happiness are doors to the supernatural—but joy and bliss are. We share pleasure with the animals. Happiness raises us above the animals, just as joy raises us above ourselves.

5. Art—the style. "Beauty will save the world," Dostoyevsky. Art is the culmination of beauty. The style of the story is not extraneous, not an accidental addition. It's a crucial dimension. We can speak of an art attack, of art that breaks hearts. Two arts that have the most power to do so: music and storytelling.

Aristotelian poetics sets out the following:

- Plot (*mythos*)
- Re-creation (*mimesis*)
- Release (*catharsis*)
- Practical wisdom (*phronesis*)
- Ethics (*ethos*)

These *five* are the enduring functions of storytelling. Our lives are marked by temporality, finitude, which gives significance to our past, present, and future. Our life, to some extent, is pre-plotted, inscribed in context, culture, class. But biography (our story) will always be more important than our biology (genes). *Mythos* is the work of telling through a crafted structure: life as *poiesis* and play. Stories have plots that unfold in *four* phases:

1. A preparatory time
2. An initiating event or calling that begins the journey

3. The journey itself

4. The return

At any moment, there may occur a reversal (from good to bad fortune, for example). Northrup Frye—the master of literary criticism—classified myths into *four* basic plots:

- The Comic or Lyric plot—here human desire feels itself overcoming the forces of human dread. Its happy characters are blessed with luck and the delightful surprises of Springtime.

- The Romantic plot—here desire has mastered dread, not by luck but by courage and strength of character.

- The Tragic plot—here dread begins to mount over the forces of desire. It is Autumn.

- The Ironic or Satirical plot—here dread reigns supreme over desire and all hope seems lost. It is Winter.

These major plots can attune us to the mysteries of everyday life, but we must listen with a critical ear.

Mimesis captures the *eidos* (idea) or essence of our lives. Action is cumulative or oriented. Life is lived while stories are told. Twentieth-century French philosopher Paul Ricœur outlines the circle of triple mimesis in *Time and Narrative*:

- The *prefiguring* of our lifeworld (*Lebenswelt*) as it seeks to be told

- The *configuring* of the text in the act of telling

- The *refiguring* of our existence as we return from narrative text to action

Il n'y a pas hors du texte: there is nothing outside the text, meaning, there is no meta-narrative. *Mimesis*, so, is a creative re-telling because there will always be a gap between reality (that which is) and representation (how I conceive of it). Stories alter us—such is the power of *catharsis* (attitudinal alteration), resulting in release (relief). They provide us with the opportunity "to feel what wretches feel" (*King Lear*): vicarious imagination, so. Stories offer us the freedom to behold all kinds of happenings and by being narrated, the harm (fear) is mitigated. *Mimesis* detaches us from the action of the play or book, permitting us to grasp the meaning of its entirety. It de-worlds us, enabling us to see the terrible, troubling, and tender truth of things; it moves us to pity (empathic detachment). Drama demonstrates alterity—shows us the other's perspective. Phronetic understanding occurs in the overlapping and intertwining of history and story. Stories encourage the sharing of common experiences, as the familiar encounters the foreign. The storied self grows in moral understanding. We are subjects of narrative—of our own and others. There is no neutral narrative—all views are views from somewhere; no view is from nowhere. "What does this text mean?," is not confined to authorial intention (the Romantic fallacy). Narrative is an openended process of poetical and ethical responsiveness.

Story is the transition, so, from nature to narrative, to time enacted and enumerated. Human life is a story of events. "Story, Rory?"—when someone asks you who you are, you tell them your story. You recount your present in the light of the past (memory) and the future (anticipation) as you recall (the past) and dream (the future). By so doing, you're offering a *narrative identity*. Storytelling humanizes time by transforming it from impersonal fragments into a pattern and plot. Life is in search of narrative—the unity of a life, as narrative provides us with a source of identity.

Storytelling is indispensable to life, be they in the form of myth, epic, sacred history, legend, saga, folktale, romance, allegory, confession, chronicle, satire, novel. Each genre shares a common function—someone telling something to someone about something (i.e., hermeneutics). There are four aspects present: a teller, a tale, something related and a recipient. The intersubjective model of discourse constitutes the communicative act. Even in Samuel Beckett's *Krapp's Last Tape* or *Happy Days*, when the author is talking to himself, there is always the implied or implicit other.

"Once upon a time" speaks to us of our origins (*arche*), just as "they all lived happily ever after," speaks to us of our end (*telos*). Stories are framed by birth and death. In-between is a world of imagined possibilities. Stories were seen as gifts form the gods. Indeed, one of the earliest roles of the shaman or sage (in Ireland, the *seanchaí*) was to tell stories, thus providing symbolic solutions to contradictions which couldn't be solved otherwise (empirically, logically). In the process, reality is transformed. Nature imitates narrative.

Myths express our yearning for the Great Escape, as Tolkien tells us. Where do we come from? Where are we going to? Are we human or divine? Are we strangers, gods, or monsters in Irish philosopher Richard Kearney's words (and book with the same title)? The great tales give relief and afford immense pleasure; they entertain and educate. They instruct and enchant.

They have the power to hush a crowd and still a room. "Wait until I tell you." Children crave bed-time stories, full of fantastic creatures and conflicts, from Grimm's fairy tales to Tolkien's *Lord of the Rings* so they might metabolize their own experiences through imaginary events. Fantasy is the ultimate buffer against harsh reality.

Our earliest myths (primordial narratives) were recreative. Myth was the most common form of early narrative—orally and trans-generationally transmitted. Stories had a sacred ritual function, be they Greek, Indian, Babylonian, Persian, Chinese, Greek, Celtic, Germanic, or biblical. We come to know Western cultural identity through the tales of Odysseus, Abraham, and Arthur. Mythic narrative mutates into historical or fictional. Herodotus and Thucydides describe natural rather than supernatural events. They kept it "real," and this gave rise to biography and case-history. By contrast, fiction re-described events through tales of romance, allegory, or metaphor. The impulse here is to narrate "as if." Then the modern novel (novel = new) emerged in the post-Renaissance period, with its synthetic power, drawing from lyric, drama, epic, and chronicle—personal voice, presentation of action, depiction of heroes, description of empirical detail. The novel evolved and was experimented with; now we have digital communication in cyber culture: from TV talk-shows to chat rooms on the internet, Zoom, Skype and the World Wide Web. What both historical and fictional narrative have in common is their mimetic function—they mirror reality. Aristotle defined *mimesis* as the "imitation of an action," by which we re-describe the world. *Mimesis* is linked to myth—*mythos* and *mimesis* as narrative's dual role.

Stories show us a different world—invite us to see our own in a new way, through a different lens, so we can imagine otherwise and experience a *catharsis* of our emotions of pity and fear—a purgation of the passions. We empathize with the characters, and we distance ourselves too from the enfolding events. Aristotle confined the cathartic power of narrative to fiction and poetry; they alone reveal the universal structures of human existence, so the *phylomythos* (the lover of myths) was also a *phylosophos* (a lover of wisdom), more than the historian was. We also interweave fact and fiction. Nietzsche famously proclaimed that all truth was fiction, and all fiction, interpretation. Stories matter. We need their power and their poetry. Could we say that the unnarrated life is not worth living?

In postmodern literature, we get play, pastiche, and paradox: invention and innovation in literature and language. Joyce remarked: we only invent what has happened. And in relation to the Gospel stories, we can say that the stories recounted are true, and some of them actually happened! The language of Sacred Scripture is lyrical not literal. To take Gospel stories seriously is not to take them literally. The imaginary and the real collapse, fuse. As Oscar Wilde wryly and wittily observed: there were no fogs in London before Cézanne painted them. Art permits us to see into the truth of things. Art, be it painting, poetry or prose, heals, transforms. Freud found this with the talking-cure of psychoanalysis. In therapy, the suffering subject recalls and recounts their lived experience. They free-associate as they *lie* on the couch, filling in the gaps in memory, as much as they can, given the lapse of time, screen-memories, and the trauma of the events. For Jacques Lacan, Freud's French disciple, psychoanalysis is a cure through speech. The early Freud took childhood memories literally (the seduction-theory); only later would he abandon such realist claims and hold it was virtually impossible to distinguish between fact and fiction (fantasy), deriving from the unconscious. All this gave rise to the False Memory Syndrome debate—the question of validity, suggestion, repression and recovered recall came to the fore: veracity versus virtual reality. Therapy locates itself somewhere between story and history. Behind every clinical case-history is a life-story: life in quest of narrative. And the concomitant demand that the stories of survivors (especially of abuse) be heard and not muffled or ignored. Of course, the chapter doesn't end—to some extent, there is no closure so long as we keep the conversation going. There is no cure, only new styles of speech, different ways of talking: thus, narrative truth—the narrative function of a life, as Ricœur calls it. Our stories relate our experiences, but we tell them from somewhere—from our lived history, through the prism of our own projections. Empirical "evidence" still has to be interpreted: from scientism to semantics and story. The story matters less than the narrating of it, which takes place like a dream. Talk is therapeutic, emancipatory. Examples of which include, Augustine's *Confessions* and Marcus Aurelius' *Meditations* (exhortations to himself). If good stories are those that can be re-told, great stories are those that can be remembered.

In *On Stories*, Richard Kearney cautions against a meta-narrative which would explain everything (but this is part of the postmodern suspicious of the "grand narrative"), which he sees as fundamentalism (it need not be) and the danger of disintegrating it into a medley of relativistic micronarratives (any language-game is as good as any other). We need to avoid the pitfall of saying that all narratives are bound to the self-referentiality of language and make no truth claims (reducing speech to simulacra and semblance) on the one hand, and on the other hand, we need to beware of what I call narrative nihilism which says, "After Auschwitz, poetry is no longer possible," resisting any attempt to say the unsayable. Surely there is an ethical function to storytelling which ensures that we don't repeat history, even if the full telling of it is impossible? If there is no one correct over-arching narrative, surely there are (consensual) compelling ones that are more convincing (some criteria, in other words)? We need to discern when it is proper to remember and when to forget, when to let go, to bow to the past but not be bound by it (Bosnia, Rwanda, Northern Ireland) and when to commemorate the past, while avoiding triumphalist commemorations. Brian Friel, the Irish playwright, once remarked: "to remember everything is a form of madness." Every society, after all, constructs itself as a story, that is forgotten it is one, be it Catholic or Protestant, Unionist or Republican (to take Ireland's example). All societies are founded on myths. Totalitarianism (and its concomitant of fundamentalism) says "my way is the only way." A Catholic example of which is "*extra ecclesiam nulla salus*" and Papal infallibility, while on the Protestant side, we have inerrancy of Scripture. One says the Pope can't be wrong (*ex cathedra*), the other that the Word of God can't err. Literalism has done much violence in terms of committing a catalogue of textual abuses. Stories are narratively constructed and can be deconstructed and reconstructed—there has to be a space for symbolic representation. Narrative, in short, can't afford to be naïve. There will always be a conflict of competing interpretations, which hermeneutics will attempt to arbitrate and adjudicate, ploughing a midcourse between *anamnesis* and amnesia, suspicion, and affirmation.

Myths open up imagination; they can lead to liberation or perversion (bigotry, racism, fascism etc.), to false consciousness and ideological distortion. We need to de-mythologize and re-mythologize, argues Kearney, in a double gesture, as stories incarcerate (idols of bewitchment) or emancipate (symbols of enchantment). What we are presently witnessing in the United States and the United Kingdom is a populist nationalist narrative which is intent on homogeneity and cultural hegemony—the rejection of alterity and universality, and therefore unity. Sectarianism is a long-told story of subjugation and slavery, as official and unofficial (anecdotal too) stories vie, and facts become commingled with "alt-facts." Democracy is always daunting and in danger of disintegration.

The myths of our cultures (archetypes) express in metaphor our experiences. We recognize ourselves in these archetypes, be it the *Great Gatsby*, the Count of Monte Cristo, the Scarlet Pimpernel—there is usually one story that provides the central meaning of our lives. We live our personal story (unique) against the backdrop of a universal narrative (archetype). Archetypes (these universal psychical structures) are reflected in symbols and images common to all cultures and times. They are universal algorithms which recur in art, fairy tales, myths, and dreams. The classical myths are stories in philosophical form. Mythology is philosophy's prehistory. Myths deliver messages of meaning; they are civilization's foundational stories, bearers of possible worlds. Mainly myths deal with order—with bringing gods and men who transgress back to harmony. Pride (*hubris*), which is regarded as immoderation, is punished. The greatest virtue is *dike*—justice (right measure). The Delphic temple's (shrine to Apollo) injunction to "know thyself" meant knowing your limits (boundaries), your natural place in the grand scheme of things, avoiding arrogance and achieving wisdom ("nothing to excess"). We can highlight *three* such moral messages emerging from Greek myth:

- *Cosmos*—the harmonious order of the Whole/All

- *Dike*—justice: agreement/attunement with the order of things

- *Hubris*—resistance to immoderation for purposes of balance and right order in the soul and society

What ancient mythology bequeathed was that the twin evils that weigh upon human existence are: nostalgia and hopefulness. If the former is attachment to our past, the latter is anxiety over our future. Both are snares. They prevent us from living in the present and become the permanent focus of our fears. Such apprehension is the great obstacle to the good life. Myths bid us to accept our fate (*amor fati*) but also urge us to protest when something is wrong (an act of rebellion).

If extraverts talk in order to think and introverts think in order to talk, both tell stories. Without stories we would have no way to symbolize, let alone understand the truth spoken in love. Every story can be told in multiple ways. Only in telling stories, do we make history. There are *four* key components to any and every story:

1. Hero—saves the day (leader has vision)

2. Guide—right-hand man (mentor)

3. Dragon or monster (lies between the hero and the treasure)

4. Treasure—justice, prosperity for all (universal salvation)

In terms of one's brand-story in business, for example, we can ask:

- Who is telling the story?
- Why is the story being told?
- When and where is the story taking place?
- Who are the people in the story?
- What are the people trying to achieve? (challenges)

Be an open book. In *Lord of the Rings*, Frodo and Sam are trudging across Mordor on the heroic quest to destroy the Ring of Power. They put the greatest of all existential questions of the meaning of life into concrete terms: "I wonder what kind of story we're in." Life is a story. The key: to make of life a great story. An analogy here will prove useful: in order to be a morally good act, an act must be right in all *three* of its dimensions:

1. The act itself
2. The motive
3. The circumstances

To be a healthy human body, a body must be healthy in all of its organic systems: the nervous system, the digestive system, the muscular system, the circulatory system etc. To sum up: every story has these *five* dimensions:

1. The Plot
2. The Setting
3. The Characters
4. The Theme
5. The Style

Let's apply the Big Five to the story of our lives:

1. History—is about the *Plot* of our story
2. Physical Science—is about the *Setting* of our story
3. Psychology—is about the *Characters* in our story
4. Philosophy and Religion—are about the *Theme* of our story
5. Art—is about the *Style* of our story

Symbols

We symbolize our lives through stories. Such symbols resonate in the depths of the human psyche. We are in need of a symbolic life lest life become banal and boring and is felt as flat. Symbols signal a vast, more creative energy, a more expansive and expressive space. Symbols are particles buried in one reality which bespeak their connection to, or with, a another one. There is an intimate link between symbol and psyche. Ritual, symbol, and psyche connect, coalesce. C. G. Jung enquired: "Where do we live symbolically?" His answer: "Nowhere, except where we participate in the ritual of life." A symbol is an affect-laden archetypal image. It's something that represents, stands for or suggests something else.

The word is derived from the Greek *symbolon* meaning "token" or "watchword"; it is an amalgam of *syn* meaning "together" and *bole* meaning "a throwing." Thus, "throwing things together" is the meaning of symbolism. We gather what is scattered. Campbell describes a symbol as "an energy-evoking and directing agent." A symbol shows a double aspect. Science is the province of signs not symbols; the ineffable can only be sensed. Symbolism, by contrast, is the province of art, religion, and philosophy. The philosopher Ernst Cassirer described man as a symbolic-making animal, rather than Aristotle's description of the human being as a rational animal. A transcendent reality is mirrored in myth and symbol. Symbols are metaphors reflecting something which remains inscrutable. They hold the mind to truth but are not themselves the truth. They possess multiple levels of possible meaning. This separates symbols from signs, as signs have only one meaning. The meaning of the symbol is not inherent in the symbol. A sign stands for something known; a symbol stands for something unknown, to be more precise, for a known unknown.

Symbols are found in dreams, myths, and legends. They fulfil crucial psychological functions. Paul Tillich, the Protestant theologian, said that symbols always point beyond themselves. They have a depth dimension. They are complex. But a symbol can lose its power and become "dead" or be reanimated and become "alive" again in the consciousness of man. The danger is literalism, as we said: to take the symbol for the reality. And literalism can lead to fundamentalism. The unique nature of a symbol is that it gives access to deeper layers of reality which are otherwise inaccessible. We need symbols and rituals to give meaning to life. Their transcendent energy touches us and draws us, permitting us to see life *sub specie aeternitatis—* under the auspices of eternity. The essence of an initiation experience, for example such as one finds in Freemasonry, is to permit the person to move into contact with symbols. Unfortunately, in modern times we have lost touch with dramatic rituals and rites of passage and initiation ceremonies. The symbolic life is encountered in rites and rituals. Now, a rite is a formal act, and a ritual is a set order for the carrying out of rites.

Initiations correspond to *hinge* experiences. Like hinges on a door, they permit the possibility of passage from one room/dimension to another; as such, they are creative events which create connections—linkages between things.

Symbols and icons both represent other things, but an icon is a pictorial representation of the product it stands for, whereas a symbol does not resemble what it stands for. A symbol represents an idea through an image; an icon represents a visible item. A symbol is subjective in that it requires interpretation.

Symbols see everything as metaphor. Symbols destroy fossilized dictionary definitions, opening the doors of perception and imagination, permitting us to see something *as*. This "seeing-as" is the essence of symbolism.

The Path of Poetry

Poetry is the privileged site for symbolic language. It transcends politics and history, to some extent—if it is not propaganda. Some poems entertain, while others educate. Some are didactic, others more descriptive than prescriptive. Reading and relishing a poem is more than an experience—it is an event. Poets are prophets. They are priests who read the signs of the times and unwittingly perhaps signal the spirit at work in the world. Poets creatively tap into a vast spiritual storehouse of energy and by so doing enliven our own lives and elevate us. Poetry's place is sometimes societally on the margins of meaning—it's always uncertain as it takes us out of the world of consumption and production. Poetry evokes, provokes.

Prehistoric man created poetry in Africa as far back as the 25th-century BC. The earliest epic was the *Epic of Gilgamesh* written in Sumerian. If Aristotle tried to describe and define poetry in his *Poetics*, as we mentioned, distinguishing between the epic, the comic, and the tragic, Plato, for his part, had banished the poet from his ideal *polis* (as he was thrice removed from the truth), thus sparking the ancient quarrel between poetry and philosophy. Romantics such as Keats would insist that poetry is an attempt to render the beautiful and sublime without the burden of engaging in logical or narrative thought processes—Keats' famous "negative capability" was intended to designate a person capable of being in uncertainty and ambiguity, in mystery and doubt "without any irritable reaching after fact and reason." Coleridge and Wordsworth likewise praised the power of human imagination. Wilfred Bion, the British psychoanalyst who influenced Samuel Beckett, elaborated on Keats' term to illustrate an attitude of openness of mind—the ability to tolerate the pain (and pleasure) of not knowing.

If prosody studies meter, rhythm, and intonation, we can say that poetic form is more flexible in modernist and postmodernist poetry. Painting is visual poetry. There are sonnets and villanelles; there are Limericks, Odes and Japanese Tankas, narrative poetry, lyric poetry, epic poetry, satirical poetry, elegy, fable, dramatic poetry, prose poetry, light poetry, slam poetry (developed since 1984 whereby commentators speak aloud on personal and social matters), and RAP (rhythm and poetry), which combines rhyme and street vernacular: a case of Kanye West proving more popular than Wordsworth, and Eminem and Drake proving more apposite than Eliot and Dickinson.

If modernism emphasized the creative role of the poet in the process, postmodernism stresses the role of the reader of the text. All reading is relative just as all translation is a form of textual terrorism that does violence. To move through life is to navigate it narratively in a world that requires translation itself. It is always possible to translate otherwise. Something is always *leftover* and left out—a remainder.

All texts have contexts, be they poems, paintings, railway tracks, boxes of matches or the human being ("I can read you like a book"). Meaning reveals as much as it conceals; language is polysemic and equivocal. When we read (or hear) great poetry, we read ourselves reading the poem. Poetry opens up what prose pegs down. Language is the House of Being, Martin Heidegger remarked. The poet weighs each word. His utterance refers to his inwardness, to what pertains to the soul. The poet shows, hints at something elusive. Poetry is Saying ("poetry moves in the element of saying"). Language touches the innermost nexus of our existence. The poet is mindful of language and meets the thinker halfway in thought. The poet's vocation is a call to the word as source. Poetry and philosophy need each other. If poetry is song, song is existence (Hölderlin). Poetry transports us to another world and in the process, we are transmogrified.

Poetry plumbs the depth of soul and expands the horizon of our world. Words disclose worlds of meaning.

"What are poets for?," asks Heidegger in *Poetry, Language, Thought*, in our destitute times, when the divine radiance has become nearly extinguished. But the poet's word keeps the trace of the Holy: poetry as prayer thus. Poets *dare* language. The venturesome are the Sayers and the Sayers are the poets *par excellence*. It is a Saying other than the rest of human saying. And that is why we need our poets; they are custodians, guardians of the word through which we may hear the rustle of the divine breath. We mortals live in the speaking of language even when it is the language of silence. Poets *care*; they show concern for speaking, for saying. "Poetry," as Heidegger puts it, "is what really lets us dwell"; " . . . poetically, man dwells . . . " on this earth.

Good poetry, like all great art, reveals the divine aura of things, suggests a superabundance of transcendent meaning. Art is "self-justifying joy," as the philosopher Bernard Lonergan once remarked. Art is liberation. It points to the Beyond of things. Poetry provides us with an experience of *elemental meaning*. It is embodied, nonconceptual meaning—one that moves us. Art is thus the expression of an experience of elemental meaning: a spiritual, everyday epiphany. Poetry is the privileged path to moral and even religious conversion as we orient ourselves to the true, the good and the beautiful. Hopkins and Herbert, Dickinson and Donne, Rilke, and Rumi, to name but a few, gesture in the direction of the groundless ground of being, and attest to the truth of transcendent meaning. The true purpose of poetry is to help us to (re)discover the ultimate source of love—the surplus of sense in the depths of divine reality. We then see the world as a sacramental sign revealing transcendence in immanence, and the timeless in time. Poetry and painting witness, in a privileged manner, to the eternal Mystery.

Lost in Translation

If we translate a poem, we come to inhabit a different world—one dwells in alterity momentarily. There is no utopian or total translation that offers a perfect replica of the original. Translation, as Ricœur notes in his little book, *On Translation*, is always *after Babel*. There is a multiplicity of tongues, a polyphony of voices. To read a text is to "work through" it; to translate one is to forever renounce the illusory dream of pure correspondence. Where there is language, there is interpretation and translation too. All translation is a dialogue between self and stranger. When one translates one receives the word of and from the Other. Translation is the exchange of narratives. To think and speak is always to translate. There is the tireless transference of appropriation and misappropriation between texts—mine and the Other's, opening up an ethical space of interlinguistic hospitality. Translation is always incomplete, the work of an unfinished business, which is *telling*. The translator's task is to relinquish a hoped-for equivalence. He must, so, surrender to some loss and sense of invincibility. For there is the vow of fidelity to the work/word and the reality of its betrayal. Poetry, especially, presents the serious difficulty, Ricœur observes, of the inseparable combination of sense and sonority, of the signified and the signifier. The semantic field is full of boobytraps. There is the impossible task of serving two masters: the reader and the author; and the effort to bring the author to the reader and the reader to the author. There is gain yes, but not without loss, what Ricœur calls "equivalence without adequacy." All translation fails inevitably. The gap between cannot be filled. But this chiasmus does not leave us forlorn but, rather, full of home for the irreducible play of language. As George Steiner once remarked: "to understand is to translate." Truly, translation is the work not only of memory and mourning but of tentative understanding rather than totalized explanation. Translation makes clear that every perspective is partial. And why we're always trying to make ourselves understood. There is, of course, the unspeakable, therefore, the untranslatable. As Derrida might have put it: translation is impossible and that's why we must make the impossible that bit more possible. Difficult? Yes. Impossible? No. A "good enough" (to employ D. W. Winnicott's term) translation aims at a supposed equivalence, an equivalence without identity. There is not just the renunciation inherent in translation but the *risk* of translation too. We may have to surrender all notion of what Ricœur calls the "comfortable shelter" of the equivalence of meaning. Is this a shame? A disgrace? We may never measure up to the level of the letter nor count on a word for word translation but *the construction of a comparable* is worthwhile work, caught as we inevitably are within the confines of the hermeneutic circle, one that is not vicious, however, but stimulating and alive with promise.

Duende

A *duende* is sometimes depicted as a creature in Latin American culture who helps show the path home to people who have lost their way in a forest. "*Tener duende*" (to have *duende*) is a Spanish term for a heightened state of emotion and expression. *Duende* is the spirit of evocation, akin to *daimon* (demon/spirit). It arises from inside one and emerges as a physical-psychological response to great art, especially to that poetry written in blood. It's what gives you chills, and makes you cry or smile. Lorca had developed the aesthetics of *duende* in a lecture he gave in Buenos Aires in 1933 entitled "*Juego y teoría del duende*" ('Play and Theory of the *Duende*'). *Duende* seizes one, captures and ensnares, viscerally. For Lorca, *duende* is a power, a struggle that climbs up from the soles of one's feet. It's not a question of style but of blood and dark music, which no philosopher can explain or unravel. It scorches the heart. It embraces the pain of love and the play of melancholy. All love songs contain it; none quite capture it. It haunts one. You find it, for example, in the lyrics of Bob Dylan and Leonard Cohen. All arts are capable of *duende* but none more perhaps that those which spring from the soil and soul of Hispanic culture.

Amid the mellifluousness, music and meter, the song and sibilance of the verse, poetry leaves a splendiferous stain upon the silence of the world. Heidegger hints at a possible hymn to meaning and mystery when he muses with a gentle wisdom: "In the poet's song, the word appears as the mysterious wonder."

4

Styles of Speech

IN THIS CHAPTER, WE will look at two personality profiling models which can be used to discover one's speaking style and way of communicating: the DISC model (briefly) and the Enneagram system (in more detail). Personality is complex and intricate, especially so when one considers there are 7.6 billion people on planet earth with their own ways of thinking, behaving, and communicating.

The DISC is popular, straightforward, and standardized. It's a four-factor model developed in the early 1900s which helps to identify behavioral patterns. The Enneagram is far deeper and dates back more than a thousand years. It and can be deployed not just in terms of personality typology but also spiritual transformation.

DISC

The DISC model is based on the work of psychologist William Moulton Marston who developed it. It was developed to classify people and help them understand each other better, especially with regard communication. The roots can be traced back to the ancient idea of the four elements: earth, air, water, and fire, upon which Empedocles drew. Hippocrates postulated the existence of four temperaments: choleric, phlegmatic, melancholic, and sanguine. Galen contributed to and continued this type of theorizing. The choleric personality was said to be strong-willed and ambitious (fire), the phlegmatic was patient and calm (water), for example. In the twentieth-century, Hans Eysenck offered a bi-axial model of mapping and C. G. Jung explored psychological typology with a model that influenced the Myers-Briggs inventory, with the two attitudes of extraversion and introversion plus the four functions of consciousness: thinking, feeling, sensing, and judging, while DISC, for its part, centers on *four* personality traits:

1. Dominance
2. Influence
3. Steadiness
4. Conscientiousness

D refers to how you find solutions to problems; I refers to how you relate to others; S refers to your energy level and pace; and C refers to how you respond to procedures and rules. One can take a test to find out one's DISC profile (as well as Enneagram type). In terms of the D, I, S, or C personality types:

D: aims at accomplishing results; emphasizes the bottom line; sees the big picture; can be blunt; accepts challenges; gets straight to the point; motivated by winning; competitive; successful; achieves immediate results; direct; demanding; determined; forceful; strong-willed; self-confident; values personal freedom.

In terms of speaking and communicating with a D personality, one shouldn't ramble or pad one's speech with purple prose; stay on task; be blunt, specific, clear, and prepared; no chit chat, present material efficiently; focus on the facts; give them the bottom line, be brief; avoid generalizations; focus on solutions not problems.

I: aims at influencing and persuading others; demonstrates openness in relationships; enthusiastic; optimistic; collaborates well; dislikes being ignored; convincing; magnetic; trusting; warm; takes action; decisive; motivated by social recognition; fears loss of influence; impulsive; disorganized; lacks follow-through.

With I personalities, talk to them about their goals; support them; give them time to relate; encourage them to stay focused on the facts; share your own experiences; avoid overloading them with details; don't interrupt; use words like "impressive" and "inspiring"; refrain from being too factual; offer them incentives and rewards. The I personalities are optimistic, collaborative, animated and vocal—they like to get attention.

S: aims at cooperation; sincere; dependable; does not like to be rushed; calm; supportive; patient; predictable; deliberate; stable; consistent; overly accommodating; fears change and offending others; values loyalty and security. The S personality can put one in a good mood; calm, approachable, supportive, level-headed; they don't like being rushed.

When communicating with an S, be personal and amiable; express interest in them; clarify; be polite; don't be rude, aggressive or confrontational; draw out their personal goals; minimize emotional language; be persistent and diplomatic.

C: aims at accuracy, expertise and competency; independent; objective; rational; detailed; fears criticism and being wrong; accurate; challenge assumptions; careful; cautious; systematic; diplomatic; tactful; generalizes.

When communicating with a C, focus on the facts and give details; minimize preparatory talk and emotional language; be patient, persistent, and diplomatic. The four compass points of personality yield *twelve* different combinations:

1. The Challenger (DC): assertive, driven, accomplished, perceived of as aloof, insensitive, informal, creative, confident.

2. The Winner (D) is also a dominant type (like DC): demands results, needs to slow down, has raw energy.

3. The Seeker (DI): creates ideas and opportunities, is bold, brief, and direct in their communication, innovative, needs to be more self-aware.

4. The Risk Taker (ID): bold, idealistic, risk-taker, frustrated at slow pace of others.

5. The Enthusiast (I): extravert, passionate about different things, high energy, inspires others, overactive mind, will-power, neglects to listen sometimes.

6. The Buddy (IS): empathetic, good listener, confident, approachable, perceptive, kind.

7. The Collaborator (SI): brings people together, good listening skills, effective with teams, collaborative, dependent.

8. The Peacekeeper (S): steady, reliant, credible, considerate, peaceful, trustworthy, not a team player or risk-taker.

9. The Technician (SC): logical, works quietly, doesn't interact much, determined.

10. The Bedrock (CS): reliable, responsible, withdrawn, lacks confidence.

11. The Analyst (C): seduced by details, loses track of time, perfectionistic, focused, insightful.

12. The Perfectionist (CD): assertive, attentive, driven, clear, difficult to live with.

The statistics in relation to the percentage of the population who identify as D, I, S, or C, are:

D: 3%

I: 11%

S: 69%

C: 17%

The Enneagram

The Enneagram is a powerful model of the psyche which is principally taught as a typology of nine interconnected personality types. It is an ancient and accurate system and especially pertinent for effective communication as it enables one to understand the behavior and speaking styles of the nine types, which is crucial. Each enneatype has its own lens or filter to perceive the world. By coming to understand the nine types we get an idea of how each type converses with others.

Source: Integrative Enneagram Solutions

The following is the list of the nine types (and different descriptions have been used):

1. The Perfectionist
2. The Giver
3. The Performer
4. The Romantic
5. The Observer
6. The Loyal Sceptic
7. The Optimist
8. The Boss
9. The Mediator

Speaking Styles

Each enneagram type has a default style of speech. There are, therefore, *nine* distinct ways of communicating, according to the system, depending on what type we are. We can access other styles but when we're coasting on automatic pilot, we tend to drift into a default style.

Ones

Ones are accurate and detail oriented. They are responsible, well-organized, diligent, and steadfast. They perform tasks methodically and tend towards careers in academia, finance, forensics, law, and the military. They are perfectionists and reformers who sermonize in speech. Their voices can be shrill. They have an edge to their speaking style. Ones instruct. Their grammar and pronunciation are very proper. They are often teachers or preachers. They are straight-forward, direct, and honest. They are also argumentative and think they are always right. They can be pushy, pedantic, and tedious. Ones are accurate and exact and can become obsessive and compulsive about getting the details right. They get impatient easily and stop listening. They have a sense of mission. They are inflexible and can come across as "preachy" and dogmatic, but they do think about what is said to them and may change their opinion accordingly. Ones can be hyper-critical and arrogant. Their communication style is matter of fact and deliberate, opinionated, and easily irritated. They have no problem displaying their displeasure—they use judgmental and righteous words such as "should" and "ought." They focus on meanings and have little time for small talk. They need to speak more in the service of the message rather than wanting to be right all the time. They need to know when things are "good enough," and soften their speech, as their tone is heard as intimidating and focused on rules, procedures, obligations, and operations. Theirs is the Augustinian adage: "Right is right even if no one is doing it; wrong is wrong even if everyone is doing it." To create rapport with Ones, take things seriously and join them in their effort to improve things. Avoid disregarding good manners and don't take their tendency to be critical too personally. When communicating with a One, speak with authority and conviction. Check in on them frequently as they are prone to burnout. It's good to give them feedback, direct instruction and constructive criticism. As they are self-critical, you could also help them to share responsibility, delegate, loosen up and accept their mistakes and perceived imperfections.

Twos

Twos are warm givers. They are helpers. Twos overextend and appeal to *pathos*. They are empathic, warm-hearted, attuned, approachable, kind, compassionate and connecting. Their pitfall is pride. They need to be loved, appreciated, needed, understood. "I'm giving you so much that you really should be grateful." In speaking, they can over emote, gush, and get lost in emotion so the audience gets lost or reacts. They offer facile compliments and flattering remarks. They are always ready to give advice. Their speech is supportive. Their voices are soothing and gentle (in keeping with their demeanor). Twos prefer intimate one-on-one conversations—*tête-à-têtes*. They can come across as a bit wishy-washy. They need to be humbler, use stories more, back off and be without attachment. Their language is caring; they listen carefully and ask questions. They are either overly indirect or too direct. They offer unsolicited advice. They use positive reinforcements in their speech, one which acknowledges the feelings and needs of others. To establish rapport with Twos, show approval and appreciation, and make personal contact. Avoid being too critical; be sensitive to their feelings. And don't take their flattery too personally. Twos are sensitive and vulnerable to criticism, seeing critical comments as personal attacks, so be careful in how you frame your feedback. Help them set boundaries with others and see that they can become intrusive at times. Twos need constant appreciation and can feel let down if that is not fulfilled, so an email or text can offer them the assurance they crave.

Threes

Threes are confident and charming. They are convincing performers who may come across as cocky. Threes are achievers. They are results and solutions-driven in their preparations and can sense what their audience wants. They are focused on goals. They can sell anything—the proverbial ice to an Eskimo. They are quick, smart, spontaneous, inspirational, competent, competitive, and ambitious. They set high standards; they are dead set in being number one. They are driven. They see interactions as competitions. They are charismatic and tend to make good first impressions. They tend to be well dressed, with refined tastes especially in outer appearance. They have busy schedules—they like to get things done rather than to plan too much. They desire affirmation. Threes propagandize—both themselves and their products. They speak with assurance and enthusiasm. Their communication is compulsive—they are intent on getting their message across. Their style of speech is confident and clear. They may be strong on style and low in content. They can come across as too slick and polished, however, and may not be trusted on that account. They pretend to know more than they do. They need to not cut corners and give credit to others. They don't disclose fully, often get frustrated and impatient with lengthy conversations and emotional exchanges. To create rapport with a Three, talk quickly and appreciate their work. Don't get in the way of their forward momentum and don't take their competitiveness too personally. Threes would do well to be reminded that success comes in multifarious ways and that relationships with people are equally important to working with them. Encourage them to take breaks lest they exhaust themselves in pursuit of excellence. They need to be honest with their needs and feelings and resist doing things just to be accepted.

Fours

Fours are lamenting romantics and individualists. Fours are creative and connect with their audiences. They set the mood/tone well but need to give more detail. They are self-aware and wish to be unique, hence their often bizarre or eccentric choices in fashion and general lifestyle. Fours tend to withhold themselves from others. Their speech is descriptive, dramatic as well as melancholic and full of longing; they are skilled in delivery, are creative and sensitive. They sigh frequently as if the world is too much for them. They carry their suffering on their sleeve. They speak intensely and poetically, with a certain lyricism. Their conversations are full of metaphors and flowery language. They are poetic and imagistic. They can be warm but also pessimistic. They can be too attached to their own uniqueness, though, and audiences may not relate. They can get lost in their emotion which alienates. They need to learn to use drama only to accentuate a point and be wary of separating themselves from their audience. To connect with a Four, value their emotional sensitivity and creativity and appreciate their individualism and style. Avoid forcing them to become conformist or rational. Don't take what they say when they're upset too personally. Challenge them to stay in the middle ground, avoiding wounded withdrawal on the one hand, and outbursts of rage on the other. Support them in achieving emotional balance and steer them clear of dwelling on negative thoughts. Their biggest fear is not finding themselves, so accompany them on their journey of self-discovery. Ask them about their satisfactions and current role; give them space to develop their self-esteem. Encourage them to start small with one step at a time, to bring out their full potential.

Fives

Fives are logical and reasonable. They are observers, investigators who tend to speak as if they were writing a thesis. They are inquisitive, curious, and critical thinkers. They are analytical and want to understand first causes and underlying principles. They are independent and can become isolated. They are non-conformists and are unconcerned about what's "on trend." The communication style of Fives is formal, insightful, with touches of complexity and well-thought-out responses. They give epigrammatic replies or expound with a treatise. Their speech is controlled. They are reluctant to share personal information or feelings. Their conversations focus on clarity and intention. They have a knack for simplifying complex matters. They think extensively before speaking. They mull things over. These introverts don't like small talk. Usually they don't say too much, being stingy and sparse with their communication. They say little so as not to appear foolish. They like to synthesize and summarize what others say. They can be long-winded. They generalize and rationalize and give reasons for everything. They can read the room well, are knowledgeable and accurate, but they need to work on their delivery and resist the temptation to present lots of heavy information in a sequence. They are very systematic but often have a dry sense of humor which saves them. They should tell more stories and be less "lectury." They quote too many sources, get lost in thought, come across as a bit detached and withholding. They need to watch their tendency to abstract themselves and try and put themselves more in their stories/speeches—be more present and simplify more. To create rapport with Fives, give them time to think and create an environment for them which allows them to take their time. Avoid putting pressure on them to make quick decisions or immediate contact. Don't take their withdrawn independence too personally. As Fives tend to get absorbed in their own minds, it's best to ask them for direct communication. Emphasize the importance of relationships. Above all, don't crowd them. Fives need their space. Fives find it difficult to relax so give them opportunities to unwind, for example, by creating time for exercise with which to channel their tremendous energy.

Sixes

Sixes are thoughtful to their audiences, authentic, committed, security-conscious, trustworthy but can be caught up in negative feedback and become anxious. Sixes are sceptics and loyalists who are faithful to a fault, as well as dutiful but can serve hidden agendas, are anti-authoritarian and prefer the group to the spotlight. They are rebellious and defiant. They value trust and are cautious but can become indecisive, self-doubting, and downright suspicious. Sixes are trouble-shooters. They can come across as unclear and conspiratorial. They frequently use shock tactics to get their points across and talk in short shotgun blasts. A characteristic of the communication patterns of Sixes is cautioning and setting limits. "Be careful," "mind that," "don't go too far," are frequently heard from the mouth of Sixes. They stay within prescribed perimeters and parameters. They like laws and boundaries. They can come across as overprotective and paternal. They speak rapidly, expressing their worries often. They need to define and refine their message more and slow down their speech. They also need to highlight an optimistic feature. Their language is careful and precise. They can excessively question others and become overly reactive in their responses and easily agitated and angry. They are clear, formal communicators with a warm touch; they choose their words carefully. To create rapport with a Six, agree on rules and procedures and value their attention to problems. Join them in figuring out what can go wrong before moving on. Don't withhold information from a Six or change the goalposts. And don't take their negative and suspicious attitude too personally. Avoid being ambiguous and taking on their projections. Assume they will act antagonistically when they feel threatened. Challenge them to take responsibility for their actions. Suggest mentors for them who will boost their confidence. Note that they will ask a lot of questions for reassurance. Honor their questioning. Refrain from overtly criticizing them. Sixes are realists who appear as pessimists. Don't sugar-coat the facts.

Sevens

Sevens are charismatic, energetic, and entertaining. Sevens are enthusiastic, extraverted, and optimistic storytellers. They are high-spirited. They put a positive spin on things. They have many passions and endless energy; they have many different hobbies and see the world as their playground. They have a relentless curiosity. They can't keep idle. They will often get exhausted and become both impatient and impulsive. They are highly productive—ideas flow from them at great pace. They are naturally charismatic, charming, and child-like. They desire contentment and work hard to maintain their freedom and happiness. They are great re-framers, are upbeat, fun, and adventurous. They communicate through exaggerating, embellishing, and elaborating events and experiences. Their language is positive, energetic, and expressive. Their stories savor and spice up life. Sevens are talkative and great company. They are masters of ceremony and frequently comedic. They like to please others through their speech and storytelling. They are always "into" something. Their voices soar. "Fantastic," "brilliant," "amazing," are words that pour from the mouths of Sevens. They are fast talkers, easily distracted and find it hard to follow linear sequences. They need more solidity, preparation and to not rely so much on "winging" it. They can be too attached to their stories and can make a lot out of a mundane trip to the local shop. They can appear pollyannaish and dilettantish, knowing a little about a lot but not a lot about one thing. They can skip and skim and need to be slightly more serious. They need also to learn the topic more and not get distracted and not reframe everything. They get others hyped up over things. They especially like talking about themselves. To create rapport with a Seven, appreciate them and their many ideas, have fun with them, and enjoy envisioning new possibilities. Avoid interrupting their stories and coming across as too negative. Don't take their cheery self-absorption and short attention span too seriously. Tell them what you need from them and repeat it often. Devise ways to get them to stop talking and start listening. As they are highly productive and get easily distracted, help them to make clear plans that focus their attention and utilize their wide array of skills. Refrain from forcing them into a predictable routine; don't limit their tasks. Diversify their work as much as possible. Meet their positive attitude with optimism and enthusiasm. Don't be overwhelmed by them—they don't mind that you can't keep up.

Eights

Eights command attention and are authoritative. Eights are bosses, born leaders, challengers who like to debunk and admonish. They emit a strong aura and high esteem. They are goal-oriented, assertive, and confident. They exert influence, power, and control. They are unafraid of confrontations. They believe in hard work to make things happen. They are self-reliant, dominant, and strong. They often assume leadership roles—they work to make their presence felt. They are clear, certain, direct, and straightforward as well as forceful, and honest in speech. They inspire, create large energy, and speak from the gut. They put down what they don't understand or like. They verbally squash what appears to them as weak. They protest and are against a lot of things. They can say "no" but have trouble saying "yes." They can come across as angry and dismissive. They are demanding, challenging, commanding. Their tone is firm and full of imperatives. They mean business and are bossy. They need to be more flexible, consider other points of view, soften their delivery style, be less "in your face" and pushy. They are like bulls in a China shop and too attached to their truth. They need to back up their speeches with information and facts and filter their speech through the heart, as well as doing more homework, fleshing out their talks a bit more and recognize dissenting points of view. To create rapport with an Eight, make direct contact, join them in getting work started. Avoid showing disrespect or keeping them still for too long. Don't take their aggressive attitude too personally. Be ready to receive their anger. Let them direct conversations to feel in control as this creates a safe environment for them. As Eights don't want to be controlled, make them think that something is their idea. Clarify goals, deadlines, and limitations. Offer them help because even though Eights are self-reliant, they are also loyal, protective, and devoted to those who stand by them.

Nines

Nines see all sides of an issue and points of view. They are able to relate with different audiences. Nines are conciliatory mediators—peacemakers—who merge with their audiences. They are gentle, non-threatening, comfortable, easy-going, and charming, as well as humble, kind, and harmonious. They have the likeability factor and are idealistic. But they need to work on not getting stuck on details, and on not being afraid to move outside their comfort zones to try new things. They can come across as too extraneous and extemporaneous. Their speech is rambling and appears to have no point, as they hold all perspectives without reaching a conclusion. They are laconic and monotonous in speech and can put people to sleep with their passive verbiage. Their speech lacks excitement and emphasis. There are no highs or lows in their pitch and speech patterns. Their voices are flat. They frequently indicate that they don't care or know. They speak in generalities and are lacking in specifics. They need to define their message more and resist the temptation to go on autopilot. They need to keep returning to their central point lest their audience becomes lost. We don't need to hear the whole story. Nines tend to become complacent and numb out. They are softly spoken and avoid conflict and tension. Their communication style is gentle, calm, careful, and encouraging. They are not forthcoming with their own opinions and perspectives and their speech is low in feeling tone and affect. They can become passive-aggressive to avoid conflicts and have occasional outbursts. Assure them that it's ok to say "no" to friends and colleagues alike.

The Nine Communication Styles

Ones preach, teach, lecture, and say "I ought to," and "I should." Twos compliment, charm, cajole, seduce, and ask personal questions. Threes pitch, propagandize, and advertise. Fours dramatize, engage in meaningful silences, and use words with strong feeling tones. Fives communicate via email speech, theses, treatises, and lengthy briefs. Sixes express caveats, complaints, constraints, concerns. Sevens brainstorm, hypothesis, tell tall tales, excite. Eights engage in diatribes, threaten, are blunt and uncensored. Nines meander, maunder, relate epics, sagas, are repetitive and rambling.

We can summarize the nine types and their nine speaking styles below, thus:

Type	Speaking Style
Ones: The Perfectionist	Sermonizing
Twos: The Giver	Warmth
Threes: The Performer	Convincing
Fours: The Romantic	Lamenting
Fives: The Observer	Dissertation
Sixes: The Loyal Sceptic	Apologetic
Sevens: The Optimist	Enthusiastic storyteller
Eights: The Boss	Commanding
Nines: The Mediator	Conciliatory

In short, the Enneagram would advise to:

1. Speak from your strength

2. Serve the message

And you will be heard.

Body Language

In terms of *soma* and body-language, let's summarize the somatic characteristics of the nine enneatypes.

Ones are tense, tight, and taught in their jaws, resulting from resentment and striving. They present an angular profile with pointed features. They are well-defined and well-scrubbed. Their movements are precise, perfect but also jerky. They manifest tension around the left eyebrow, frequently raising their left eyebrow when being judgmental. Ones hold themselves erect, with spine straight and stiff. Their gestures are hard. They have a neat appearance, with hair combed and shirt tucked in. Their gaze is unwavering, penetrating, and stern, their jaw clenched, with a stiff upper lip. They are neat and proper, with a rigid posture.

Twos have a more tender façade than their tauter neighbors, the Ones. Twos have less defined features. They possess a softer and rounder exterior, positively Rubenesque at times. Twos' eyes appear soft, dilated, yielding. They are sweetly seductive and adjustable to their audience.

Threes present a youthful, dynamic appearance. They are athletic and frequently tanned. They dress fashionably and like to be "on trend." They dress for success. Theirs is a smooth and polished persona. They are bright-eyed and busy tailed, eager beavers, or bedraggled from overwork.

Fours present themselves in a supercilious and aloof manner. Their attitude is haughty. They carry a sense of specialness and superiority. But this is a cover for their fear of being rejected. They appear to be looking down their noses, nostrils curling up, conveying a snooty look. Their appearance is one of studied casualness. Like good actors, they have rehearsed their parts, practiced their lines, and convey a dramatic and theatrical flair, both in voice and gesture. They are often good dancers—sleek, sensitive, and graceful in their movements. They are elegant and classy, sometimes shocking, and outrageous in appearance.

Fives look studious and scholarly. They frequently wear glasses—the result of all that reading. Their eyes are set deep in their skulls. They frequently appear pale, possibly because they are inattentive to their bodies, but they also like to be invisible like a good spy. Some Fives are endomorphs, others somewhat portly, and ectomorphic. They present as pale, sometimes patrician, sometimes nerdy.

Sixes appear worried, wary, and somewhat jowly, with their chin centered and equal tension on both sides of the mouth, their eyes narrowed looking for lurking dangers. They appear fearful, fretful, fidgety, skittish, nervous, anxious, angry, tentative, and aggressively defensive.

Sevens have a cheery countenance, with chubby and cherubic visages. Their faces are less worn and wrinkled than other types, probably because they are not overly stressed by guilt or worry. They aren't necessarily overweight (seeing as their cardinal sin is gluttony). Most maintain proper body proportions. They have bright eyes and winning smiles.

Eights can look weather-beaten and gnarled as though they have endured punishment or have spent a lot of time outdoors in the elements unprotected. Male Eights have barrel chests. They tend to be athletic in appearance, with a mesomorphic body-type. They have deep, resonant voices. Eights tend to maintain direct eye contact. There is an intensity to their glare/stare. They possess a commandeering presence which locks on to the other. They appear brash and commanding.

Nines appear as having no energy and are usually expressionless. There is a certain blandness and plainness to their features. They possess an endomorphic physique, probably as a result of their psychical indolence. They are calm and simple, appear comfy, sometimes disheveled, and unkempt.

To conclude: the Enneagram is a fascinating and precise instrument which, when deployed, can offer tremendous insight into the differences in speaking styles and body-language of the nine types and their behaviors, which is a great aid not only in conversing with each type but in avoiding confrontations with them too.

5

Compassionate Communication

"First learn the meaning of what you say,
and then speak."—Epictetus

In *The Art of Communicating*, Thich Nhat Hanh sets out the ingredients for mindful, compassionate communication, which he puts forward in *five* steps. Hanh thinks of communication along the lines of consumption. He begins by reminding us that we often ingest toxic communication from those around us as well as from what we watch and read, so we need to be mindful about what types of communication and speech we are being nourished by on a daily basis.

"Conversation is a source of nourishment."—Hanh

What we need is a) mindfulness of speaking and b) mindfulness of listening, i.e., nourishing, healing communication. The antidote to poisonous relationships is mindful compassionate and loving communication.

First, however, we must learn to communicate with ourselves. We think our I-phones help us communicate but they aid us only in so far as our speech is authentic. Talking or texting does not mean we are necessarily communicating. The most fundamental instrument in communication is the mind. Self-communication is a revolutionary act; mindful awareness is this stopping and sitting with yourself. It is full awareness of the present moment, which will help to communicate with compassion.

When Hanh says that the way in is the way out, what he means is that once we can communicate with ourselves, we will be able to communicate outwardly with more clarity. Mindful breathing promotes communication between the mind and body. Freedom is precisely this ability to stay in the present and is the foundation of happiness. So, when we think of communicating, we need also to mention "nonthinking" and "nontalking," in other words, stilling the body-mind. Self-communication is this nonthinking and nontalking. It is interior silence. We even worry about what others are thinking! When we stop thinking and talking, we begin to listen—to ourselves first, then to others. In true communication, the mind is more important than the mobile. The practice is to communicate lovingly with yourself. When we simply stop and sit, the present moment becomes available to us and we can listen deeply to the sounds of nature. The main desire in all communication should be the desire to understand—not to prove a point or make ourselves feel better. *Two* things are necessary for effective and true communication:

- Deep listening
- Loving speech

These two together produce compassion; they are the best instruments for a) restoring communication, and b) relieving suffering. Anger cannot promote compassionate communication. Connecting with one's Self, however, does. We communicate to be understood and to understand. The important thing is not to get caught up in judgement. Deep listening creates moments of happiness which help us handle painful emotions. Hanh recommends listening for thirty minutes with compassion to help the other person suffer less. This should be the main intention. When anger boils up or agitation and irritation, we lose our capacity to listen. The practice of mindful breathing and mindful walking become the disciplines required. And when we listen, we should do so without correcting or interrupting, bitterness, or blame. Understanding is the foundation of love just as compassionate communication is the language of love. Look for deeper modes of connection and communication, compassion, and curiosity. Both mindfulness and skillfulness are needed. Use words that nourish the soul. So much damage is caused by unkind, untruthful. or violent words. Loving speech is what Buddhists call Right Speech. It is open, truthful, compassionate, reconciling, tolerant, and forgiving. There are *four* elements of Right Speech:

1. Tell the truth (don't lie; if we think the truth is too shocking, we need to find a skillful way to tell it. If lying is a language-game that can be learned, so is truth-telling an art form. So, tell the truth in a way the other person can hear).

2. Don't exaggerate (refrain from inventing and embellishing, as it takes one away from both truth and trust, if practiced habitually).

3. Be consistent (no double-talk; true speech means being true to your word).

4. Use peaceful language (don't use insulting, humiliating or cruel words, condemnation or verbal abuse).

There are *four* criteria for Right Speech:

1. We have to speak the language of the world.

2. We may speak differently to different people, in a way that reflects how they think and their ability to receive the teaching.

3. We give the right teaching according to person, time, and place, just as a doctor prescribes the right medicine.

4. We teach in a way that reflects the absolute truth.

Firstly, we have to use the language that people speak. Secondly, we must speak according to the understanding of the person listening (sometimes deeper answers will be required, depending). Thirdly, we need to prescribe the right medicine for the disease, i.e., offer the appropriate teaching for that person. Fourthly, our speech needs to reflect (carefully) the absolute truth—the closest thing to a description of ultimate reality, for example, the truth of non-duality (that there is no such thing as the separate self).

In any communication, the attention should be on the mind, the tongue, and the ear. Listening deeply is looking as well as loving deeply. The four trainings in Right Speech remind one to use words that express kindness, support, and non-discrimination. Just as Right Speech brings about healing and unity, so does false or wrong speech cause hurt and ill-being.

According to Hanh, there are *six* sentences or mantras that embody loving speech, which is the practice of calm, compassionate communication:

1. First mantra: "I am here for you" (the presence of your Self, which is an act of love).

2. Second mantra: "I know you are there, and I am very happy" (the recognition of the person's presence and that it is conducive to your happiness).

3. Third mantra: "I know you suffer, and that is why I am here for you" (used when you notice that the other person is suffering. "True love is made of mindfulness").

4. Fourth mantra: "I suffer; please help" (used when you believe that the other person has caused your suffering). This can be broken down into *three* further sentences: a) "I suffer, and I want you to know," b) "I am doing my best," and c) "Please help." So: "I suffer, and I want you to know it. I am doing my best. Please help."

5. Fifth mantra: "This is a happy moment" (the realization that the present moment suffices for our happiness to be complete).

6. Sixth mantra: "You are partly right" (used when someone praises or criticizes you).

The practice of the six mantras is a way to keep the door of communication open. Of course, conflicts inevitably arise in communication. The first rule is to desist communicating when angry because we are not lucid in such states—this just escalates the situation. Rather, explore the root of the anger; get in touch with it. When one is angry at someone, it's nearly impossible to use loving speech. Pride and wrong perception can cause a lot of suffering. One must always be seeking restitution in relationships, reconciliation, and resolution. We can't wait for our parents or partners to change. We need to concentrate, instead, on our own thoughts, speech, and actions. Deep listening and compassionate dialogue can be practiced even in our legislative assemblies as well as schools and workplaces. Ask yourself: do I smile at the people I see? How do I approach meeting my friend? With a clear or closed mind? Do I have mindful meetings? We need to speak from our experience rather than engage in verbal duels. Our meditative practice and our presence can have such a powerful and positive effect on those around us.

Communication and community both share a common Latin root, *communicare*, meaning "to share" or "make common." Through our speech, we can succeed in contributing to and creating compassionate communities and a global ethic. Shared meditative silence or communal chanting creates a collective energy which can combat negative emotions and toxic feelings and thoughts. We tend to think our communication is in the words we speak or write but our body language—our facial expressions and tone of voice and gestures, are all ways we communicate. Communication is not neutral.

"Every time we communicate, we either produce more compassion, love, and harmony or we produce more suffering and violence."—Hanh

Our communication is *karma* (a Sanskrit word meaning "action"), that is to say, our continuation. Throughout the day, we are producing energies of thought, speech, and action all the time. We're communicating either with ourselves or others at every moment. Thinking, speaking, and bodily activity are our manifestations. To produce a thought is to act. We can communicate with clenched fists or open arms. Every communication bears our unique signature. What we want to produce is the best kind of thinking, the best kind of speech, and the best kind of bodily acts. Finally, Hanh proposes *eight* practices for compassionate communication:

1. The Computer Bell (a bell of meditation can chime to bring us back to awareness and away from criticizing or complaining speech).

2. Drinking Tea in Mindfulness (a time set aside to communicate with ourselves. "There is only the tea').

3. Listening to Your Inner Child (our wounded child within needs our care and attention).

4. Writing a Love Letter (a real letter addressed to someone in your life using loving speech. You will find that the person who finished the letter is not the same as the person who started it).

5. Peace Treatises and Peace Notes (two tools to help heal hurt. The peace treaty can be used as a preventive tactic. It goes like this: "I, the one who is angry, agree to:

   a. Refrain from saying or doing anything that might cause further damage or escalate the anger.

   b. Not suppress my anger.

   c. Practice breathing and taking refuge in the island of myself.

   d. Calmly, within twenty-four hours, tell the one who has made me angry about my anger and suffering, either verbally or by delivering a peace note.

e. Ask for an appointment for later in the week to discuss this matter more thoroughly, either verbally or by peace note.

f. Not say, "I am not angry. It's okay. I am not suffering. There is nothing to be angry about, at least not enough to make me angry."

g. Practice breathing and looking deeply into my daily life—while sitting, lying down, standing and walking—to see: the ways I have been unskillful at times; how I have hurt the other person; how the seed of anger in me is the primary cause of my anger; how the other person's suffering, which waters the seed of my anger, is the secondary cause; how the other person is only seeking relief from his or her own suffering; that as long as the other person suffers, I cannot be truly happy.

h. Apologize immediately, without waiting until our appointment, as soon as I realize my unskillfulness and lack of mindfulness.

i. Postpone the meeting if I do not feel calm enough to meet with the other person.

I, the one who has made the other angry, agree to:

a. Respect the other person's feelings, not ridicule him or her, and allow enough time for him or her to calm down.

b. Not press for an immediate discussion.

c. Confirm the other person's request for a meeting, either verbally or by note, and assure him or her that I will be there.

d. Practice breathing and taking refuge in the island of myself to see how: I have seeds of unkindness and anger as well as habit energy to make the other person unhappy; I have mistakenly thought that making the other person suffer would relieve my own suffering; by making him or her suffer, I make myself suffer.

e. Apologize as soon as I realize my unskillfulness and lack of mindfulness, without making any attempt to justify myself and without waiting until the meeting.

We vow to abide by these articles and to practice wholeheartedly. Signed, the _____ day of _____ in the year _____ in _____.

Peace Note

Date:

Time:

Dear _____, This morning/afternoon/yester-day, you said/did something that made me very angry. I suffered very much. I want you to know this. You said/did _____

_____

_____

_____

_____

Please let us both look at what you said/did and examine the matter together in a calm and open manner this Friday evening.

Yours, not very happy right now,

_____

_____)."

6. Beginning Anew (begin again and look deeply at your past actions, speech, and thoughts, to create a fresh beginning).

7. The Cake in the Refrigerator (this can help children deal with their parents' arguing. The practice of the cake restores harmony. Turn to the person who seems upset or annoyed and say, "there is a cake in the fridge" which really means "please, let's not make each other suffer anymore." Hopefully, they'll say "I'll go and get the cake." The person who is upset or angry has an opportunity to withdraw. Anything can substitute for the piece of cake).

8. Hugging Meditation (mindful hugging can bring about healing and happiness—it is a deep practice).

Thinking

"Most thought-provoking in our thought-provoking time is that we are still not thinking."—Martin Heidegger

"The happiness of your life depends upon the quality of your thoughts."—Marcus Aurelius

When in *Hamlet* (act two, scene two), Shakespeare said there is nothing either good or bad but thinking makes it so, he was giving prominence to our reasoning ability. Ability is what you are capable of; motivation determines what you can do; attitude determines how you will do it. Attitude is more important than aptitude. We are our thoughts: "as a man thinketh, so he shall be." Everything begins with consciousness. Thoughts, words, saying, hearing. We can chart a trajectory thus:

- What I think
- What I can put into words
- What I say to others
- What people understand

We think thoughts; we put our thoughts into words and perhaps struggle with making ourselves clear; we communicate some of these thoughts to others; then there is what people understand us as saying, which operates so very often as a missed encounter (for example, Chinese Whispers).

- Thoughts become words.
- Words become actions.
- Actions become habits.
- Habits become character.

"Character is destiny."—Heraclitus

We have been considering speech (conversing and convincing). Now let us briefly say something on the subject of meditative thinking as a propaedeutic to the next chapter, where we will conclude on a note of silence.

Martin Heidegger's *Discourse on Thinking* was published in 1959. We mentioned him briefly earlier. His little work has two parts, consisting of an address and a dialogue written from notes on a conversation dating from 1944–45 between a teacher, a scientist, and a scholar on a country path. Heidegger distinguishes between *two* types of thinking:

1. Calculative thinking
2. Meditative thinking

The former is typical of science. It is a thinking that computes. It never stops, never collects itself. It is not the thinking that contemplates the meaning of being. Meditative thinking, by contrast, ushers in a transmutation, a movement into the region of what is ultimate, characteristic of the poetry of the mystics. It profits nothing, practically speaking. It demands practice, delicate care, genuine craft. Heidegger describes man as a thinking, that is to say, meditating being, even if he has proceeded by way of forgetfulness of being. Man is that being for whom his own being is at stake. We not only wait *for*, but we wait *upon*, which is deeper. We wait, in openness to the given, for the disclosure/unveiling of Being. Meditative thinking begins within the field of awareness, but it still takes place where "objects are" (Heidegger will still talk of "the consciousness of objects"). Meditative thinking as a form of "releasement" may be existentially deeper than mere calculative thinking, but it still isn't meditation, where thinking breaks off (objectless awareness). Meditative thinking "regions" us, re-shelters, offers an expanse and an abiding, a resting. We are far from mindful thinking; indeed, we are "thought-less." Man is "in *flight from thinking*," which is the ground of thoughtlessness. In *Poetry, Language, Thought*, Heidegger suggests that thoughts come to us; we never come to thoughts. In meditative thinking, things become slow. The poet is a traveler in the land of the saying of Being. Poets venture to *say*. Their saying/singing hails the holy, bids the divine draw near. We are always speaking, Heidegger maintains, even when we do not utter a single word aloud. A poem is that which is spoken purely.

In *What is Called Thinking?*, based on a series of lectures the philosopher gave in the summer and winter semesters of 1951 and 1952 at the university of Freiburg, Heidegger names Socrates as "the purest thinker of the West"; Plato is regarded as the "greatest thinker of the West." For Heidegger, thinking is not about having an opinion or having an idea nor is thinking ratiocination. Opining, reasoning, representing, conceiving all have their place, as does science ("science doesn't think"). Thinking is a response by us to a call which issues from Being, from the nature of things. It is more a way of living, a dwelling than an activity; it is a remembering who we are (memory is the gathering of thinking that recalls), a gathering and focusing of our entire selves on what lies before us; the aim of which is to discover the thing's essential nature—its truth. Truth is the revealing of what is concealed. Thinking is a seeing and a saying of the way the world is. Thinking is inherent in man as a being-in-the-world. Questioning is a way, a path, especially of oneself. To think is to be underway. Being desires, deserves to be thought truly. The call of thought is to pay attention, to be attentive to things as they are, to let them be as they are. We have acted too much and thought too little. Philosophers are the thinkers *par excellence*.

Teaching (declared to be impossible by Freud) is more difficult than learning because the teacher has to learn to let his students learn. Thinking is our hardest handiwork. We may quote Hölderlin's hymn to Socrates:

> "Why, holy Socrates, must you always adore
> This young man? Is there nothing greater than he?
> Why do you look on him
> Lovingly, as on a god?
>
> 'Who the deepest has thought, loves what is most alive,
> Who has looked at the world, understands youth at its height,
> And wise men in the end
> Often incline to beauty" (*Socrates and Alcibiades*).[1]

He who has most deeply thought . . . Is not this the call, the character of the philosopher? Thinking is a handicraft, which involves learning listening. "Thinking is thinking when it answers to what is most thought-provoking."

The Old English word, *thencan* meaning "to think" and *thancian*, meaning "to thank" are closely related. Grateful thought so. The thought implies the thanks. Thinking (being receptive to reality—to that which is) involves giving thanks. If the supreme thanks is thinking, then thoughtlessness is the most profound thanklessness.

> "One should both say and think that Being is."—Parmenides

The essential nature of thinking is determined by what there is to be thought about: the Being of beings, which makes us marvel. Wonder. Words on the wind. Words to the wise. And staying silent, to hear.

> "Language speaks as the peal of stillness."—Martin Heidegger

Any uttering breaks the stillness. Mortals speak by responding to language in a twofold way: receiving and replying. Hearing is how we respond to language. And hearing/hearkening to the voice of Being requires silence.

> "The rest is silence."—William Shakespeare

---

1. Hadot, *Philosophy as a Way of Life,* 167.

6

Meditation and the Language of Silence

Silence

"It is a great thing to know the season for speech and the season for silence."—Seneca

WE LIVE BETWEEN SPEECH and silence. There is verbal and nonverbal communication. Our words signify, our bodies gesture. Communication is a practice, one which requires wise words as much as deep listening which is the hearing of the heart. Conversation/communication is the art of attention which provides the other person with the opportunity to speak more and suffer less. Loving speech and compassionate listening will rescue and restore us. One should never underestimate the weight of words nor the power of deep, receptive listening. Both have the capacity to transform both oneself and the other. Perhaps it's not coincidental that the word "listen" also contains the same letters as "silent." In the end, our tongues are stilled, our words fall short of the Word, and what is left is a stain, as Samuel Beckett put it, on the silence of the world. But what a stain; what a silence. As Beckett wrote in *The Unnameable*: "I shall never be silent. Never." Thus, the writer speaks. He wants to keep the conversation going. But certain things can't be spoken, only shown. This Wittgenstein knew. "What we cannot speak about, we must pass over in silence"—ineffable silence, which the movie "Into Great Silence" (2005) shows so spectacularly by depicting silent Carthusian monks in permanent prayer.

"Meaningful silence is better than meaningless words."—Pythagoras

Between Speech and Silence

In on "Restraint of Speech," which is chapter 6 in the *Rule*, St. Benedict writes: "I have resolved to keep watch over my ways that I may never sin with my tongue. I was silent and was humbled, and I refrained even from good words." So even good words may be omitted out of esteem for interior silence. "Indeed, so important is silence that permission to speak should seldom be granted" (the monks used to perform hand signals). "The disciple is to be silent and listen." The *Rule* condemns "vulgarity and gossip and talk leading to laughter, and we do not permit a disciple to engage in words of that kind." Words direct our attention and energies. St Benedict condemns murmuring in a monastery. Silence is seen as a joyful communion with the Absolute. Monks are enjoined not to look forward to speaking in the refectory but to see these times as interrupting their silence. The mystics of all ages have enjoined us to practice stillness and silence.

> "The very best and noblest attainment in this life is to be silent and let God work and speak within. Therefore, it is said: "In the midst of silence the secret word was spoken to me."—Meister Eckhart

> "There is a huge silence inside each of us that beckons us into itself, and the recovery of our own silence can begin to teach us the language of heaven. In silence man can most readily preserve his integrity. There is nothing so much like God in all the universe as silence."—Meister Eckhart

Like Eckhart the Dominican friar, Thomas Merton, the Cistercian (Trappist) monk, practiced interior silence. In *Thoughts in Solitude*, in which he acknowledges the influence of Swiss philosopher Max Picard's book *The World of Silence* on his own thinking, Merton writes: "Words stand between silence and silence—between the silence of things and the silence of our own being . . . . When we have really met and known the world in silence, words do not separate us from the world nor from other men, nor from God, nor from ourselves because we no longer trust entirely in language to contain reality. Truth rises from the silence of being to the quiet tremendous presence of the Word. Then, sinking again into silence, the truth of words bears us down into the silence of God. Or rather God rises up out of the sea like a treasure in the waves, and when language recedes His brightness remains on the shores of our own being." Sinking into silence, the Self is made manifest as the Absolute. Only in silence and solitude (the desert experience), Merton contends, can man dialogue with God. The beings who are in silence make silence real because their silence is identified with their being. "To name their being is to name their silence." My knowledge of myself in silence opens out into the silence of God's own Self. In silence, He speaks my name. Merton's life was a listening; His is a speaking. Merton's sanctity was hearing (and responding). His silence was his salvation. For silence is the stuff and substance of sanctity. In silence is formed the strength of the saints and sages. Silence is ordered to and anchored in the ultimate; it liberates us from useless words. Merton, the monk, soaked his life in spiritual stillness, turned it into a vocational and vigilant silence.

"Meditation is one of the ways in which the spiritual man keeps himself awake."—Thomas Merton

In his book, *Silence*, Buddhist monk Thich Nhat Hanh, argues that we need silence in order to hear the call of life and love, and that mindfulness is the particular practice that stops the noise inside, ceases the internal chatter of the mind. There is a radio playing in our head which he calls Radio Station NST: Non-Stop Thinking. By contrast, mindfulness sounds as a bell that reminds us to stop and silently listen. This is *noble silence*— it's establishing a silence within myself. Such a *thundering silence* frees me from mental chatter. Silence is the sound of no sound. Hanh sets out what he calls *five* "true sounds":

1. Wonderful Sound—the sound of birds and rain etc.

2. Sound of the One who Observes the World—this is the sound of silence, of listening.

3. Brahma Sound—this is the transcendental sound, *OM*. ("In the beginning was the Word," *John* 1:1; a "big bang").

4. Sound of the Rising Tide—the voice of the Buddha.

5. Sound That Transcends All Sounds of the World—the sound of impermanence.

Daily concerns are all the activities with which we are consumed during the day. *Deepest* concerns involve us existentially with ultimate concerns. When we have silence within, we can find some answers to philosophical questions such as, "Who am I?" Meditation stills the mind. It is much needed in the steady daily diet of noise. There seems to be a fear of silence. We are either talking or taking in something, be it texts, television, or thoughts.

They occupy a space within us—a veritable smorgasbord of stimuli. We consume *four* kinds of food. The Four Nutrients are:

1. Edible food—food you eat with your stomach.

2. Sense impressions—the sensory experiences you receive through your ears, nose, tongue, body, and mind. This includes what you hear, read, smell and touch.

3. Volition—this is your will, concerns, and desires (it feeds your decisions, actions, and movements).

4. Consciousness (individual and collective)—the way your mind feeds itself.

These foods can be:

1. Healthy (nourishing)

2. Unhealthy (toxic)

This will depend on what you consume. We leave the doors to our consciousness open most of the time and are invaded by the sounds of the world and by suffering. Conversation is sensory food. We consume what we give our attention to. The choice is ours as to whether we want to consume toxic or healthy consciousness, brutality, or beauty. Internal dialogue/discourse consumes our thoughts, distracts us. We are our thoughts (and feelings etc.). Hanh distinguishes between store consciousness and mind consciousness. The former is like the basement of a house. Seeds are stored here and whenever one is stimulated (watered or triggered) it comes up from its dormant/latent state and manifests on the level of mind consciousness, where it's no longer just a seed but a zone of energy (mental formation). It can take over the living room/space, becoming an unwelcome guest difficult to lodge. We need to water the wholesome seeds and practice *not* to water the seeds of fear or hatred or craving.

> "Just as a candle radiates light, heat, and scent, our thinking manifests itself in various ways, including in our speech and our actions."—Thich Nhat Hanh

The thoughts we produce carry the energy of our feelings. To cultivate interior silence, we can walk or breathe mindfully; we can pause throughout the day. Even just stopping in our tracks for a few seconds can succeed in shutting out our mental machinery. This *spacious* silence is far removed from the *strained* or simmering silence of people who don't know what to say next to each other. Silence doesn't just mean not talking, is not simply the absence of speech. The silencing of our speech as well as thoughts refreshes, restores, renews. Tablets, television, and texts, media sites and mobile phones all clamor for our attention. Silence, by comparison, comes from the heart. It really means we're not disturbed inside, no longer perturbed by constant inner, idle chatter. Unless we still the mind, talking will continue on inside. Inner strength comes from such luminous silence.

> "Silence allows for deep listening and mindful response, the keys
> to full and honest communication." —Thich Nhat Hanh

Am I overlooked or overloaded? Am I speaking just to speak—to say something, anything? Do I listen to what's being said? Do I spend some time alone in solitude, in silence, still, in the cell of my heart? Or am I caught up, captured by endless words?

> "The heavens do not say anything." —Confucius

Our essence is wordless. We need a "sound pause" rather than a "soundtrack," a monastic bell to break from the ceaseless stream of stimuli. Stillness is the profound power of presence, which brings us into the present, into awareness. When we meditate, we enter what Hanh calls the "island of self." It is harbor, homecoming, compassion, connection, true communication. The music of loving silence nurtures our spirit. Even in music, there are moments of rest, of no sound. Real solitude comes from a calm heart rather than a forest hut, as we sit just to sit, and silently sound the sacred mantra.

> "Let silence take you to the core of life." —Rumi

> "Silence is the language of God. All else is poor translation." —Rumi

We are told by Plato many times in his dialogues that Socrates stood still until dawn in silence, and in some dialogues (*Critias* and *Timaeus*), he has become altogether silent. Socrates's silence in the *Timaeus* signals the withdrawal of philosophy itself in the face of a discussion of the origins of creation. Socrates, who loved conversing through dialectic, signals to us that silence is the true form of speech. Similarly, for St. Thomas Aquinas, the last word was not conversation but silence. His tongue, at the end of his mortal life, was stilled by the superabundance of his life in God. Thomas is silent, not because he has nothing more to say, but because he has been shown the inexpressible depth of mystery beyond all speech. Silence is shown to be the place of thinking, of thinking silence. "Man speaks by being silent" (Heidegger). Socrates's and Thomas' silences are like receptacles, *choras*, receptive spaces into which they receive all the stories to come, all the words that will flow and spill about them. As Beckett's Molly remarks in *The Unnameable*, one needs courage "to go silent." "Where I am, I don't know, I'll never know, in the silence you don't know, you must go on, I can't go on, I'll go on." A dead silence, thus, which may be contrasted with Emerson's "wise silence." Emerson will argue that within man there is the soul of the whole, the universal beauty, to which every part and particle is equally related, the eternal One.

> "There is a two-fold Silence—
> sea and shore—
> Body and soul. One dwells in lonely places,
> Newly will grass o'ergrown; some
> solemn graces,
> Some human memories and tearful lore,
> Render him terrorless: his name's No More."—Edgar Allan Poe,
> from "Silence—A Sonnet"

"Man teaches us to speak. The gods teach us silence."—Plutarch

By way of example, Josef Pieper, the Thomist philosopher, researched the great Goethe. Nothing surprised him more (he tells us in his little book *The Silence of Goethe*) than how much of Goethe's life was spent in seclusion, how much this seemingly communicative man who carried on a world-wide correspondence never wanted to expose through words the core of his existence. It was Goethe's essential silence that made the strongest impact on Pieper, who concludes his find with this summation:

> When such talk, which one encounters absolutely everywhere in workshops and in the marketplace—and as a constant temptation –, when such deafening talk, literally out to thwart listening, is linked to hopelessness, we have to ask is there not in silence—listening silence—necessarily a shred of hope? For who could listen in silence to the language of things if he did not expect something to come of such awareness of the truth? And, in a newly founded discipline of silence, is there not a chance not merely to overcome

the sterility of everyday talk but also to overcome its brother, hopelessness—possibly if only to the extent that we know the true face of this relationship? I know that here quite different forces come into play which are beyond control, and perhaps the *circulus* has to be broken through in a different place. However, one may ask: could not the "quick, strict resolution" to remain silent at the same time serve as a kind of training in hope?[1]

Like Socrates, Goethe's silence is the silence of one who listens. Such listening or meditative silence is like a breath, penetrating the innermost chambers of one's soul, revealing the transcendental truth that the meaning of being silent is hearing. This Grand Silence is heard in monasteries. The chief function of monastic silence is the presence of the *memoria Dei*. In the desert, monastic silence represents a protest against propaganda and idle talk, reminding us of what is essential. Interior silence links all meditative paths and practices. It offers a clearing of the mind wherein one can hear the voice of the Absolute. If speech is the organ of this present world, then silence is the mystery of the eternal world. As Iris Murdoch has one of her characters say in her novel *Under the Net*: "All artists dream of a silence which they must enter, as some creatures return to the sea to spawn."

T. S. Eliot describes the power of silence beautifully in his iconic poem "The Rock":

The endless cycle of idea and action,

Endless invention, endless experiment,

Brings knowledge of motion, but not of stillness;

Knowledge of speech, but not of silence;

Knowledge of words, and ignorance of the Word.

He proceeds to ask: Where is the wisdom we have lost in knowledge and where is the knowledge we have lost in information.

"Only in silence, can one remain in truth."—Ludwig Wittgenstein

Meditation

"To realize the Self is to be still."—Ramana Maharshi

1. Pieper, *Silence of Goethe*, 28.

> "Compose yourself in stillness, draw your attention inward and devote your mind to the Self. The wisdom you seek lies within."—Bhagavad Gita

Meditation is the practice *par excellence* which allows us to be still and to be silent. Here I would like to highlight the importance of being present, being still, and being aware, drawing on ancient wisdom and the perennial philosophy. Practicing the pause, paying attention, and giving time to meditation are *three* essential exercises recommended for mental health and psycho-spiritual development.

- Pause between activities
- Pay attention; become more aware
- Let the mind fall still in meditation

We worry and ruminate endlessly. We get worked up about things that may not even happen in the future, and torture ourselves by way of imaginings. Such is the power of "anticipatory anxiety" that we hardly ever live in the present. We are either recalling some event from the past or anticipating some experience in the future. We thus miss out on what's happening right now under our nose. Being in the present is the ultimate antidote and answer to anxiety. What we don't attend to ceases to exist after a time.

> "The present alone is our happiness."—Goethe

> "Give yourself a gift: the present moment."—Marcus Aurelius

Application of the Senses

The senses only work in the present, so when we connect with the senses, we are *de facto* in the present. The peace of the present comes, not from the objects of the senses *per se*, but from the connection, from the act of attending itself.

> "You become what you give your attention to."—Epictetus

We have five senses: Sight (the most dominant), Sound (the most refined), Smell, Touch and Taste. When we are experiencing anxiety or anger or even having a panic attack, breathing and the senses can come to our aid.

First, just begin to breathe slowly and deeply, inhaling for three seconds and exhaling for five. Wriggle your toes (this will help to keep you grounded). Next, begin to notice your surroundings. Apply the five senses to anchor you in the present moment. It is said that when the wise walk, they just walk and when they sit, they just sit. Do the one thing necessary. Meet the need of the moment. No more. No less. Become more aware. Carry out tasks mindfully. Put the direction of your attention outward, away from the ever-active and unrelenting ego. What counters obsessive, crippling anxiety is attention to reality as it is. Being attentive involves holding a loving gaze upon an individual reality. The fullness of attention is the fullness of rest.

"Attention is the rarest and purest form of generosity."—Simone Weil

Example

Pay full, not forced attention. Attention involves "unselfing." To give an example from philosopher Iris Murdoch. Picture this. You are in your study brooding to some damage done to your prestige and you suddenly become aware of a kestrel hovering outside the window. You turn your attention in the direction of the kestrel—open and out. At that moment, *all is kestrel*. Everything is changed, your consciousness charged with new energy. A Gestalt shift has occurred. And when you return to your books, everything seems altered, different somehow. One's hurt vanity and wounded pride—the source of the unruly upset—is now no more.

"Perceive without reverie."—Simone Weil

1. Walk outside and start looking around you, especially at natural objects such as leaves and flowers, clouds and trees, or sunsets and seas. Just observe the scene. See the detail. Focus. If you are inside, you could look at a photograph or an artwork. What do you notice? What catches your eye? Describe the light, the shadows, the contours, and colors.

2. Hear the sounds around you, to the birds singing and the wind whistling, to the dogs barking and the children playing. Or choose some appropriate music to attend to. Mozart calms the mind. You want to bring yourself to stillness. What do you hear? Describe the orchestra of noises.

3. Smell wood or petals or oils such as Lavender or Frankincense. Pour it on your skin or pillow. Allow the perfume to fill your nostrils. Describe the fragrance.

4. Drink a glass of water or cup of tea. Taste some nutritious food. Chew slowly. Savor. Relish. Describe the taste.

5. Touch a surface; feel the texture be it rough or smooth. Or squeeze a stress ball. Pour cold water over your wrists or pulse points. Describe the sensation.

"Delight in the present."—Marsilio Ficino

Acknowledge:

1. *Five* things you can see

2. *Four* things you can touch

3. *Three* things you can hear

4. *Two* things you can smell

5. *One* thing you can taste

"Meditation. Teach it to children. Even sitting still will help."—Iris Murdoch

The Pause

Sleep gives rest to the body but the Pause between activities gives rest to the mind and spirit as we separate a group of actions out if only for a few seconds. For example, if you're carrying shopping to your car, when you get into your car, simply pause before turning the key in the ignition. Immediately, begin to notice what is going on around you.

During the day, we can practice pausing, deferring desires momentarily, enlarging the gap or interval between doings, inserting a wedge which enlarges the aperture. We do this because consciousness is consumed by desire. And this space is a place of no-desire, of simply being. Dissatisfaction with the present and desire for something different in the future perpetuates unhappiness. The moving mind pursues pleasure, chases it down. The still mind, by contrast, finds happiness everywhere—it doesn't have to hunt it. Meditation is one way of engaging with a more prolonged pause, and in a more systematic and structured fashion.

- Just find some quiet place where you won't be disturbed.
- Sit straight but relaxed, upright not uptight.
- Find a balanced position. Tend to your posture and poise.
- Close your eyes.
- Breathe slowly, rhythmically.

Everything begins with the body. If the body becomes still, there is no reason the mind won't follow. Check your posture: the knees should be below the pelvis, the hands resting on the lap or palms facing up while resting on the thighs. One way of meditating is by repeating a word (mantra), sounding it within, which aids in stilling the mind, or by just observe your thoughts and feelings—what arises—without becoming attached and without judgement of any kind, and letting them gently go. One sits in the silence for fifteen minutes at the beginning, extending this practice, in time, to two sessions of fifteen, then twenty to thirty, minutes per day—one in the morning and one in the evening. Meditation is the master-key to experiencing peace. We try to become immobile, finding that unity within where there is no activity or agitation, anger, or anxiety. In such deep rest, the whole being is recharged and renewed. Stillness is the real experience of meditation.

The 4 Rs of Meditation

1. Resist no thought
2. Retain no thought
3. React to no thought
4. Return to the mantra or sacred word or breath
   (depending on the type of meditation)

Meditation is the journey home to the Self, to pure being, silent, serene, and still.

"The spirit can never be sick."—Viktor Frankl

Awareness Exercise

First, find a balanced position of the body.

Let the mind be free of any concern or preoccupation.

Let the body be still.

Be aware of where you are now.

Feel the touch of your feet on the ground, the weight of the body on the chair.

Feel the touch of the clothes on the skin.

Feel the air on the face.

If they are open, let the eyes receive color and form without any comment.

Be aware of the sense of smell.

Be fully here.

Now be aware of hearing.

Let sounds come and go without comment.

Let the hearing extend right out to the furthest and gentlest sounds, embracing them all.

Simply rest in this awareness for a few minutes.

Attend to everything with consciousness; claim nothing. Don't be concerned with emotional upheavals. Let all attention go to the work at hand, to whatever it is which you are doing right now. There is no action at the center of a wheel; but all action originates from the hub.

Mantram

"Nothing in all creation is so like God as stillness." —Meister Eckhart

Aside from set times during the day when we meditate, we can also repeat a saying or sentence from Sacred Scripture or mantra throughout the day, to anchor our agitation.

A mantram is a secret, sacred word or utterance, a numinous sound, a spiritually meaningful syllable. A mantram creates a vibration, a reverberation. In Sanskrit, *man* means "to think." *Manas* is the moving mind and *trai* means to "set free from." Mantra and mantram are the same: "to cross" or "transcend the mind." But the mantram is not about one set time and place; it can be practiced anytime and anywhere. The aim is to quieten the mind and produce inner calm. It's a mental pause.

Christian Meditation (popularized by Irish Benedictines John Main and Laurence Freeman) and Transcendental Meditation (TM) both operate by way of sounding an interior mantra. There are many other types of meditation (one such is Centering Prayer), but for now I will confine my comments to mantra meditation as the two methods mentioned above are among the most widely practiced worldwide—they are not the only two, needless to say, which deploy a mantra.

Consciousness is the dynamo of all mantras. The spiritual teacher Eknath Easwaran describes *eight* points in the process:

1. Meditation—the silent repetition upon meaningful inspirational passages from one of the great world religions.

2. The mantram—silent repetition of a holy name or hallowed word from one of the great world religions.

3. Slowing down—reduce hurry and stress.

4. One-pointed attention—give full concentration to the matter at hand.

5. Training the senses—enjoyment of simple pleasures with measure and without excess.

6. Putting others first—loving service.

7. Spiritual companionship—good company (*satsanga*).

8. Reading the mystics—Sacred Scripture.

Repetition of the mantram during the day manages stress and reduces symptoms of PTSD. The mantram operates by way of a spiritual hold or anchor, which facilitates living in the present, bringing the attention away from the object of disturbance/desire. *Two* things cause stress:

1. Speed/hurry (rushing rather than resting)

2. Multi-tasking (too much to do and too little time to do it in)

We are bombarded, besieged (and beleaguered) by constant interruptions on our attention and information overloads.

If meditating in this style, one chooses a traditional mantra such as *Maranatha* (used in Christian meditation) or *Rama* (used by Gandhi) or *Shanti* ("peace"). The advice given is not to make up one's own and not to change it. Repeat it silently to yourself during the day, especially when anxious or angry or upset. Deploy it when needed and when not needed.

Practice

These are the suggestions given by the sages in relation to mantra-meditation. Give momentum to the mantra at the beginning of your practice. It should start at a fast pace/speed. Let it come to rest of its own natural accord. When driving a car, we let our foot off the accelerator not the brake. The mantra journeys with us but the mantra can stop as long as there are no thoughts in the mind. Everything feeds on attention. Engaging with the thoughts (even if they are productive or positive) is a distraction. Just attend to the mantra—this is the one thing necessary. If we let "." designate a little thought and "●" a big Thought, our meditation practice might look something like this:

```
. . . . . . . . . . . . . . . . . . . ● . . . . . . . . . . . . . . . . . . . . . . . . . . . . . . . . . . . . . . .
● . . . . . . . . . . . . . . . . . . . . . . . . . . . . . . . . . . . . . . . . . . . . . ● . . . . . . . . . . .
. . . . . . . . . . . . . . ● . . . . . . . . . . . . . . ● . . . . . . . . . . . . . . . ● . . . . . . . . . . . . .
. . . . . . . . . . . . . . . . . . . . . . . . . . . . . . ● . . . . . . . . . . . . . . . . . . . . . . . . . . . .
```

We might think "am I doing this session/period of meditation right?" Let "M" denote this particular intrusive thought concerning the practice of meditation, thus:

```
. . . . . . ● ● ● . . . . . . . . . . . . . . . . . . . . . .M. . . . . . . . . . . . ● . . . . . . . . . . . . M
. . . . . . . . . . ● . . . . . . . . . . . .M . . . . . . . . . . . . . . . . . . . . . . . . . . . ..
```

We could even name our top ten thought play-lists! Just notice these distractions, these ants (mosquitoes) in the mind, but don't let yourself be disturbed by them. Let the rhythm of the mantra carry you. Merge with the mantra. Stay in the silence, in the wordless word, that was in the beginning. The aim: great total immobility, profound stillness. The energy that emerges/arises from meditation will be *Sattva* (serene, positive attitude, peaceful, balance, harmony). *Sattva* is constructive and creative, luminous, light. Then all your actions which proceed from this state will be carried out with great ease and great economy. The following quotes from Shakespeare and Marsilio Ficino sum up the essence of meditation:

"Let be."—William Shakespeare

"You are running to seek your friend. Let your feet run,
but your mind need not."—Marsilio Ficino

"Let us not be moved or distracted by many things, but let us remain
in unity as much as we are able, since we find eternal unity and the
one eternity, not through movement or multiplicity, but through
being still and being one."—Marsilio Ficino

Meditation is nothing more nor less than the art of being oneself (one Self).
The body, eyes, and mind all come together in meditation. In the profound
stillness and silence there is only "One without a second," and that is the Observer Self. The Self is consciousness. Meditation provides the opportunity
for a deep cleanse through the light of the Self that removes dirt/impedi-
ments/excrescences (our personality traits which cover up our true nature
or essence). We can see the image of the sun in water but when there are
ripples in the water the images appear to be quivering. The quivering, however, is in the water, not the sun. The Self is like a pivot point, the hinge of a
door. The hinge remains steady just as the door swings. Electricity pervades
the entire power network of a city. The intensity (voltage) at the source remains stable and unchanging, even if the current (stream of electric energy),
which flows along the wires is continually changing.

Meditation enables us to rise above our ego—the "I" as separate self.
It does so through the mandate of the mantra/sacred symbol. One becomes the witness to all our changing feelings, thoughts, and decisions.
The witness (and wisdom) is the stillness. Creation is like a play, like a
puppet show. Someone is pulling the strings. Meditation brings us backstage, enabling us to see what's really going on. We can then enjoy the
show with detachment; no longer will we be (over) identified or involved
in the drama. We become Self-realized. The Self is eternal, is consciousness, is happiness, is truth. The Self is the source, the sun within, and the
sustainer. A conscious person comprehends a lot more than the eye can
see. Someone sitting in a moving train mistakenly thinks the motionless
train is also moving, when in fact it's not. Stillness is the real experience of
meditation (one-pointed attention); the mantra is but the means. Meditation is a golden thread connecting us to the source. It's like shooting an
arrow—one has to keep pulling back the bow. The stillness of meditation which counters internal riots is carried in all our subsequent activity.

Only when the mind is stilled can attention prevail. The Absolute is always available just as the sun is always there, even though clouds can cover the sun. For example, electricity is conducted through wires. The energy of electricity flows only when the switches are turned on. The energy is always available, but we need to turn on the switches to get united with the energy. Meditation turns on the Sattvic switch.

> "Men are continually seeking retreats for themselves, in the country or by the sea or among the hills . . . . Yet all this is the surest folly, for it is open to you, every hour, to retire into yourself."—Marcus Aurelius

In meditation, we release the attention from its attachment to thoughts and feelings and sensations. It's a practice of letting be, letting go, surrender, action through non-action, doing by non-doing. Meditation leads us to a deeper place in the mind where there is no thought or compelling imagery or even experience. It's akin to deep sleep. We become aware of pure consciousness. So, we can distinguish *four* states: sleeping, dreaming, waking, and Self-consciousness (the bliss of boundless being). Frequently, one's perception, especially of time, changes. We're used to thinking like this:

$$\text{Birth} \longrightarrow \text{Death}$$
$$\rightarrow$$
$$\text{Passing time}$$

Somewhere along this line, we are NOW.

$$\text{Birth} \longrightarrow \text{NOW} \longrightarrow \text{Death}$$
$$\rightarrow$$
$$\text{Passing time}$$

But each moment is NOW.

$$\text{Birth} \rightarrow \text{Now} \rightarrow \text{Now} \rightarrow \text{Now} \rightarrow \text{Now} \rightarrow \text{Now} \rightarrow \text{Now} \rightarrow \text{Death}$$
$$\rightarrow$$
$$\text{Passing time}$$

As T. S. Eliot put it: "Time past and future. Allow but a little consciousness. To be conscious is not to be in time." The present moment stays the same. It's like the wheel of a bike which turns more rapidly at the circumference while the center remains still. Meditation brings us nearer to that still center, to a greater awareness of the ever-present moment, the eternal, naked NOW. In the silence, the divine Self speaks. Sometimes the stillness/emptiness becomes a fullness.

We are personality (ego) and essence (Self): the outer and the inner. Personality is well established by the age of three. Each of us is an atom (microcosm) of the Self of the entire universe (macrocosm). We can outline *seven* steps to the supreme Self:

1. Good actions carried out with attention

2. Good thoughts: positive attitude

3. Decrease in grumbling, in complaining and criticizing and inner chattering

4. The energy of *Sattva* begins to dominate

5. Less of an identification with/attachment to worldly attractions

6. Less absorption with material success, while observing one's obligations and duties

7. Freedom from egoic preoccupation

Most of what troubles us comes from looking at the wrong end of the line of attention—at our fickle, fluid self. "Me, myself and I": everything that says "I" (the separate self) is a fiction and a fraud. The ego is constructed on the line of a fiction. The roving, rowing mind is not happy. Truth and happiness are salient features of the divine Self in all of us, that kernel of our souls (*imago Dei*).

Satchitananda

To draw on the language of Vedic philosophy:

SAT: I AM. Every created thing *is*, is some aspect of the Absolute (Creator). Who am I? I am not my volatile feelings, my turning thoughts, my conflicting, changing desires, likes or dislikes.

CHIT: KNOWLEDGE of what I am.

ANANDA: Be HAPPY (blissful) in knowing that I am.

Satchitananda: consciousness, knowledge, bliss: the *three* faces of Godhead/ the Trinity (Father, Son, and Spirit).

Energy

> "Energy is eternal delight."—William Blake

When we use energy with attention, we release it and store it up. There are *three* sources of energy, according to Advaita: *Rajas, Tamas,* and *Sattva. Rajas* is movement, activity. *Tamas* is lethargy, inertia. If *Rajas* is active and *Tamas* reactive ("to every action there is always a reaction"), *Sattva* is being (rather than doing); it's waking up. The sign of *sattva* is renewed energy. Meditation enables us to rise above the play of the three *Gunah,* which is the act of becoming one. To meditate is simply to be, to be one . . . without a second. The Self is all we are; we just don't know it (ignorance/ illusion—*maya*). We've to give up the notion that the world based on the *manas* mind, and the senses is the only world.

The *Philokalia* (which means "love of the beautiful"), which is a collection of texts written between the fourth and fifth centuries by spiritual masters of the Orthodox Christian tradition, identifies *four* stages of identification:

1. Impact: Impressions fall upon the mind. They are indifferent; there is as yet no identification.

2. Uniting: The attention is attracted to a particular set of impressions and forms a guilty union with them. If one is watching one's attention, one can see this early stage and free oneself.

3. Merging: Here the attention has merged with the object and the person has lost his identity (the individual merges with the universal).

4. Passion: Sin, suffering, sadness. The person returns again and again to the object of his desire/identification like a drug addict.

We've to guard against consenting to mental captivity. Coming to stillness is the key and discerning the pull (rather than the push), the draw (rather than the drive) which comes from the highest source with us. By paying attention to it we climb the steps to Self-realization, which is nothing less than the ladder of life. Meditation is the pearl of great price. It's the laying aside of the load that is on your mind, for two half-hours daily. When we are still (internal immobility), we are no longer prisoners or puppets, buffeted by external events. The present moment connects us to the Self (*Param-Ātman*), so that we take no thought for the morrow. The Ultimate Observer is ever present. In meditation, we begin to be who we are.

Imagine, if you will, a hand with the index finger folded against the thumb. In this symbol, the index finger represents the individual ego bowing down before the Self, and the other three fingers symbolize the three Gunah. The individual must rise above the law of the three Gunah. In this index finger (ego), there is much *Rajas*—we point the finger at someone in annoyance or accusation. This rajasic finger reprimands. The Self is here, there, and everywhere. In the Absolute-*Ātman*, there is no time or space—it is all One. The present moment is the immanent-transcendent Absolute. The light of the Self falls on the present moment, where there is no fear or worry. If in activity we are in *Rajas*, and in sleep we come under the influence of *Tamas*, in meditation we are in *Sattva*. Meditation produces/increases the supply of *Sattva*. Particles of *sattva* proliferate, pervade, permeate the being.

We need rest for body, mind, and spirit. Just as a bird has two wings, we have *two* dimensions to our existence: the material and the spiritual. *Rajas* and *Tamas* use up the energy of body and mind; *Sattva*, by contrast, is a light Guna. If we compare the three Gunah to a building we can say that *Rajas* is brick, *Tamas* is steel, *Sattva* is glass. A human being has these *three* components: the Sattvic person is centered; he moves into the second room of the building (his being) for work (*Rajas*) and the lowest room for *Tamas* (sleep). We need to use all three rooms. Sleep gives rest to the body (*Tamas* predominates). Meditation is the full rest of *Sattva*. The *three* aspects of mantra-based meditation are:

- *Japa*: the meditative repetition of the mantra
- *Dharma*: proper practice
- *Yoga*: unity

The Good is holy silence, eternal rest. The mantra brings activity to an end; it transports us to the blissful isle of the blessed, into consciousness itself—one's true Self. The mantra is the vehicle that takes us into the realm and region of pure peace and presence. It's a journey into the Absolute. Here there is only one without a second—*Ātman* himself. To be one without a second is *advaita*, where there is no *ahankaram*.

Self-Enquiry

In the *Timaeus*, Plato asked the following question: "What is *that which always is* and has no becoming, and what is *that which is always becoming* but never is?" We can state the difference thus: being (that which is) and becoming (the world of the senses which is ever changing). Water in a green bottle may look green (through the senses) but it is in fact transparent (as we know from experience).

Being → Knowledge: Reason: Truth

Becoming → Ignorance: Belief: Opinion

There is unchanging Being which is true ("I am") and there is changing Becoming which is illusory ("I am-ness"). If the former describes you in your essence, the latter describes you in your ego. For example: I am a doer, a someone or something. I walk, work, etc. I am awake, asleep, sad, small (individuality/identification).

- Observe these identifications with yourself.
- Record them during the day.
- Observe the thoughts, feelings and sensations that come and go.
- When calm, become aware of the Seer/Silent Witness who observes all these comings and goings, these fluctuations in the mind. The Seer abides in its own nature.

Five Types of Knowledge

1. Right knowledge: direct cognition (e.g., seeing a scene); inference (fire from smoke); testimony from authority (wisdom).
2. Wrong knowledge (seeing a mirage—not based on its own form).
3. Imaginary knowledge (fantasy).
4. No knowledge (deep sleep).
5. Past knowledge (memory).

Five Causes of Suffering

1. Ignorance

2. Feeling of I

3. Liking

4. Disliking

5. Fear of death

Ignorance of one's true identity leads to "I am-ness," which leads to attraction and repulsion and the fear of death.

- Observe these five tendencies in yourself.

- Record some of them during the day.

- Spend one evening alone in silence. Be aware of what's going around you and in you. Record what you discover.

One overcomes suffering through friendliness, compassion, gladness, and equanimity. We have at our disposal *four* instruments:

1. Body—the way of action.

2. Mind—the way of knowing.

3. Heart—the way of devotion.

4. Speech (say "I am not just this physical sensation, thought or feeling— it is only a temporary fluctuation/impression though it seems to rule the being." Sound this interiorly: "I am eternal, pure, and free"—*Nitya śhuddha vimukto'ham*, in Sanskrit).

Conclusion: Three Practices

Platonic philosophy may be viewed as much more than an intellectual exercise. It is a cleansing of the mind from error and false knowledge and a freeing of the soul from mere opinion. By way of conclusion, we can commend *three* disciplines (*askesis*):

- *Mananam*: the process of "reflecting," "considering," examining, meditatively and philosophically.

- *Samālocana*: "balanced vision": this involves seeing the matter under discussion from both sides, allowing the third element/aspect to emerge beyond the two (pros and cons, his perspective and mine).

- *Sadhana*: daily spiritual practice. So, observe when you are adopting a set or strong position on a subject, holding a cherished personal belief. Impending indicators include:

  - Agitation in the mind or body

  - Attachment to your point of view

  - Desire to win

  - Reluctance to listen to other perspectives

  - Holding on to an unreasonable position

  - Criticism of other people present

  - Harboring a sense of "I am right" or "I know better"

Truth must be the priority. Record your observations in a journal.

By disengaging from and transcending turbulent, troublesome, trenchant, and truculent thoughts as well as volatile emotions that are blockages to the cultivation of a luminous awareness of pure presence, profound peace is experienced by and in the being. Depression dissolves. Anger and anguish abate. The land of liberation and light loom large. In short, meditation is rest with the Self. It is the experience of unity when the individual (ego) conjoins with the universal (immortal Self/Absolute/Ātman). Grace and effort, heart and head, discipline and devotion, love, and knowledge. Everything, ultimately, is of the Absolute.

Sit quietly and hold the awareness. Let whatever comes to mind, come. Spend five minutes with this statement below. Record how you feel and what you've realized.

"Be still and know that I am God."

"Be still and know that I am."

"Be still."

"Be."

"Man's unhappiness comes of his greatness; it is because there is an infinite in him, which, with all his cunning, he cannot quite bury under the finite."—Thomas Carlyle

"He said, "In the midst of hate, I found there was, within me, an invincible love. In the midst of tears, I found there was, within me, an invincible smile. In the midst of chaos, I found there was, within me, an invincible calm. I realized, through it all, that in the midst of winter, I found there was, within me, an invincible summer. And that makes me happy. For it says that no matter how hard the world pushes against me, within me, there's something stronger—something better, pushing right back." —Albert Camus

Meditation is the way to stillness, but this stillness becomes real only in movement, as we seek to bring it into all our activity and become, in T. S. Eliot's felicitous formulation, "the still point of the turning world." Meditation effects change on both the physical and subtle realms. A beautiful poem by Mary Spain entitled "The View" sums up how the experience of stillness and silence can bring the being to unity. In our *chintina* (reflection), let us bring forth the fruit/truth of these words which can echo or operate in us as an all-prevailing sound: "I am eternal, pure, and free." *Om paramātmane namah*: To the supreme Self, a bow.

Appendix: Discourse Theory

JACQUES LACAN, THE FRENCH psychoanalyst, developed his well-known psychoanalytic discourse theory in 1969, possibly as a response to the social unrest of May 1968 in France.[1] Discourse (*discours*) refers to a point where speech (*parole*) and language (*langue*) intersect. The four configurations showing relative positions are:

1. The agent—the speaker of the discourse
2. The other—what the discourse is addressed to
3. The product—what the discourse has created
4. The truth—what the discourse attempts to express

The four terms are:

1. The subject
2. The master signifier
3. Knowledge
4. The *objet petit a* (o-object).

The four types of discourse or social bond are:

1. The discourse of the master—the know-all
2. The discourse of the university—the knowledge handed down by an institution

1. See Lacan, *Le Séminaire*.

3. The discourse of the hysteric—the common mode of speech which does nothing other than demand (especially posing the question: "who am I?')

4. The discourse of the analyst—who keeps silence and scans the subject's unconscious speech, parapraxes (slips of the tongue), lapsus etc.

Discourse refers to the trans-individual nature of language; speech implies another subject. We have *four* algebraic symbols:

1. S1: the master signifier—the dominant discourse of the community or culture

2. S2: knowledge (*savoir*)—knowledge of the time

3. $: the barred/divided subject—the person is always incomplete. We never know who we are

4. *a*: the *objet petit a* (surplus *jouissance*) or, in English, the o-object: the little object/other that causes/mobilizes my desire (e.g., the look of the Other).

The discourse of the master is dominant; his speech masks the fact that he is a divided subject like everyone else. The fantasy perpetuated is that he is whole, complete, knows what he is talking about. The Master puts the slave to work. Here we think of men against women or employer over employee. The discourse of the university is occupied by the hegemony of knowledge, especially science, but behind so-called neutral knowledge is hidden power and mastery. The discourse of the hysteric is divided, pathologized; it is the discourse where the symptom occupies a place. The discourse of the analyst is one that causes desire in the Other; it is the discourse of truth, of learned ignorance. It occupies the place of dummy, the dead one, of the subject supposed to know.

Speech is a symbolic exchange: the gift of the word. But words don't mean what they mean; there is a sliding or slippage of the signified under the bar of the signifier. Meaning operates only retrospectively. For example, if you listen to me you can't make out if I'm saying "ice-cream" or "I scream." The context dictates the meaning. There is an unstable relationship between signifier and signified, as words are arbitrary, conventional signs. So /bat/ can mean an instrument for playing a game or refer to the winged creature who comes out at night.

And all speech is demand—that someone speak back. Drawing on Heidegger, empty speech is chatter; it's in vain—here the subject is alienated from his desire, while full speech discloses the being's desire—the truth of his existence. It's full of meaning. The analyst's task is to listen to the patient's discourse, discerning the moments when full speech emerges. Between these two extremes of conscious and unconscious speech, a whole gamut of modes of realization of speech is deployed. The aim in psychoanalysis is to articulate full speech (Freudian slips of the tongue) while *lying* on the couch: "I was talking to John the other day, I mean David." "John? Who's John?" Silences and errors—lapsus—tell a story, the story of the subject. "Rebus, it is through you that I communicate" (Lacan).

Empty speech is not the same as lying, because lying can reveal the truth. Not the whole truth, of course,—*it* can't be spoken. Telling all is impossible (tells/tell alls/tell tales/tall tales). For Lacan, speech alone is the key to truth—not (knot) any old speech but free-association: a kind of labor, a stream of unconsciousness, of non-sense.

There is no escape from the prison-house of language. Our sentences sentence us. *Il n'y a rien hors du texte* (Derrida). There is no metalanguage (metanarrative) since every attempt to fix the meaning of language must be done in language. There is no "outside" of language. There is a beyond of language—the Real—but there is no transcendental signified, no way that language can tell the truth about truth. The truth stumbles in the lie. If the other person is the guarantee of the coherence of the subject's discourse, then the falsity of this guarantee is revealed by the fact that the guarantor himself lacks such a guarantee. (All the above is according to Lacan).

One justification for having speaking subjects *lie* on a couch with the analyst sitting behind is that deprived of looking, touching, and moving, the analyst can hearken to the analysand's speech. *Shema* ("Hear" in Hebrew) *Yisrael* or the Lord's Prayer could be on his moving lips.

In the beginning was the signifier.

"It is too often forgotten that the gift of speech, so centrally employed, has been elaborated as much for the purpose of concealing thought by dissimulation and lying as for the purpose of elucidating and communicating thought." —Wilfred Bion

Bibliography

Almaas, A. H. *Keys to the Enneagram*. Boulder, CO: Shambhala, 2021.

Aristotle. *Poetics*. London: Penguin Classics, 1996.

————. *The Art of Rhetoric*. London: Penguin Classics, 1991.

Assagioli, Roberto. *Psychosynthesis: A Manual of Principles and Techniques*. New York: Hobbs, Dorman, & Co., 1965.

————. *Transpersonal Development: The Dimension Beyond Psychosynthesis*. Findhorn, UK: Smiling Wisdom, 2007.

Augustine, St. *City of God*. Translated by Henry Bettenson. New York: Penguin, 2004.

Aurelius, Marcus. *Meditations*. Translated by Gregory Hays. New York: Modern Library, 2002.

Bourgeault, Cynthia. *The Holy Trinity and the Law of Three: Discovering the Radical Truth at the Heart of Christianity*. Boston: Shambhala, 2013.

Buber, Martin. *I and Thou*. Eastford, CT: Martino, 2010.

Chestnut, Beatrice. *The Complete Enneagram*. N.d.: She Writes, 2013.

Confucius. *The Analects*. Translated by D. C. Lau. New York: Penguin, 1979.

Costello, Stephen J. *Applied Logotherapy: Viktor Frankl's Philosophical Psychology*. Newcastle upon Tyne: Cambridge Scholars, 2019.

————. *Between Speech and Silence*. Eugene, OR: Pickwick, 2022.

————. *Dynamics of Discernment: A Guide to Good Decision-Making*. Eugene, OR: Pickwick, 2022.

————. *The Nine Faces of Fear: Ego, Enneatype, Essence*. Eugene, OR: Pickwick, 2022.

————. *Philosophy and the Flow of Presence: Desire, Drama, and the Divine Ground of Being*. Newcastle upon Tyne: Cambridge Scholars, 2013.

Dennett, Daniel. *Intuition Pumps and Other Tools for Thinking*. New York: W. W. Norton, 2013.

Dickens, Charles. *A Tale of Two Cities*. New York: Dover, 1998.

Dunne, Tad. *Enneatypes: Method and Spirit*. Irvine, CA: Universal, 1999.

Easwaran, Eknath, trans. *The Bhagavad Gita*. Tomales, CA: Nilgiri, 2007.

Eckhart, Meister. *Sermons and Treatises*. London: Element, 1987.

Ellis, Albert. *Reason and Emotion*. New York: Stuart, 1962.

Emerson, Ralph Waldo. *The Essays of Ralph Waldo Emerson*. Cambridge: Belknap, 1987.

Epicurus. *Principal Doctrines and Letter to Menoeceus*. CreateSpace, 2017.

Epictetus. *The Art of Living: The Classical Manual on Virtue, Happiness, and Effectiveness*. Translated by Sharon Lebell. London: HarperOne, 2007.

———. *Discourses*. Books I–IV. Translated by P. E. Matheson. Mineola, NY: Dover, 2004.

———. *The Enchiridion*. Translated by Thomas W. Higginson. 2nd ed. New York: Liberal Arts, 1955.

———. *Handbook of Epictetus*. Translated with introduction and annotations by Nicholas White. Indianapolis: Hackett, 1983.

———. *How to Be Free: An Ancient Guide to the Stoic Life*. Translated by A. A. Long. Princeton: Princeton University Press, 2019.

Erickson, Milton. *My Voice Will Go With You*. New York: W. W. Norton, 1991.

Frankl, Viktor. *The Will to Meaning: Foundations and Applications of Logotherapy*. New York: Meridian, 1988.

Friel, Brian. *Translations*. London: Faber and Faber, 1981.

Goethe, Johann Wolfgang von. *Selected Poetry*. New York: Penguin, 2005.

Goleman, Daniel. *Emotional Intelligence*. London: Bloomsbury, 1996.

Gross, Ronald. *Socrates's Way*. New York: Penguin, 2002.

Gurdjieff, G. I. *In Search of Being: The Fourth Way to Consciousness*. Boston: Shambhala, 2021.

Hadot, Pierre. *Philosophy as a Way of Life: Spiritual Exercises from Socrates to Foucault*. Edited with an introduction by Arnold I. Davidson. Translated by Michael Chase. Maiden, MA: Blackwell, 1995.

———. *The Present Alone Is Our Happiness*. Translated by Marc Djaballah. Stanford: Stanford University Press, 2009.

———. *What is Ancient Philosophy?* Translated by Michael Chase. Cambridge: Harvard University Press, 2002.

Hanh, Thich Nhat. *The Art of Communicating*. London: Rider, 2013.

———. *Fear*. London: Rider, 2012.

———. *Silence*. London: Rider, 2015.

Harris, William B. *Restraining Rage: The Ideology of Anger Control in Classical Antiquity*. Cambridge: Harvard University Press, 2004.

Heaney, Seamus. *New Selected Poems, 1988-2013*. New York: Faber and Faber, 2014.

Heidegger, Martin. *Discourse on Thinking*. Translated by John M. Anderson and E. hans Freund. New York: Harper Perennial, 1969.

———. *On the Way to Language*. Translated by Peter Hertz. San Francisco: Harper San Francisco, 1971.

———. *Poetry, Language, Thought*. Translated by Albert Hofstadter. New York: Perennial Classics, 2001.

Horney, Karen. *Neurosis and Human Growth*. New York: Norton, 1991.

Hudson, Russ, and Riso, Don. *The Wisdom of the Enneagram*. New York: Bantam, 1999.

Irvine, William. *A Slap in the Face: Why Insults Hurt—And Why They Shouldn't*. Oxford: Oxford University Press, 2013.

James, William. *The Principles of Psychology*. New York: Dover, 2000.

Jeffers, Susan. *Feel the Fear and Do It Anyway*. London: Vermilion, 1987.

Jung, C. G. *Letters of C. G. Jung, Volume 2: 1951–1961.* Edited by Adler Gerhard and Aniela Jaffé. New York: Routledge, 1976.

Kearney, Richard. *On Stories.* Thinking in Action. New York: Routledge, 2001.

Keller, Helen. *The Story of My Life.* New York: Penguin, 2010.

Lacan, Jacques. *Le Séminaire. Livre XVII. L'envers de la psychanalyse.* Edited by Jacques-Alain Miller. Paris: Seuil, 1975.

Laird, Martin. *Into the Silent Land: The Practice of Contemplation.* London: Darton, Longman, and Todd, 2006.

Lonergan, Bernard. *Insight: A Study of Human Understanding.* Edited by Frederick Crowe and Robert Doran. Collected Works of Bernard Lonergan 3. Toronto: University of Toronto Press, 1992.

Lorenz, Konrad. *On Aggression.* London: Methuen, 1963.

Lyons, Linda. "What Frightens America's Youth? Teens Have Host of Fears." *Gallup*, March 29, 2005. https://news.gallup.com/poll/15439/what-frightens-americas-youth.aspx.

Machado, Antonio. *Poesías Completas.* Madrid: Espasa-Calpe, 1984.

Maitri, Sandra. *The Spiritual Dimension of the Enneagram.* London: Penguin, 2001.

Marston, William Moulton. *Emotions of Normal People.* N.d.: Andesite, 2015.

Milton, John. *Paradise Lost.* Alma, 2019.

Montaigne, Michel de. "On Fear." In *The Complete Essays*, translated and edited by M. A. Screech, 81–84. London: Penguin, 1993.

Murdoch, Iris. *The Sovereignty of Good.* London: Routledge & Kegan Paul, 1970.

Palmer, Helen. *The Enneagram: Understanding Yourself and Others in Your Life.* San Francisco: Harper & Row, 1988.

Pieper, Josef. *The Silence of Goethe.* South Bend, IN: St. Augustine's Press, 2009.

Plato. *Complete Works.* Edited with introduction and notes by John M. Cooper. Indianapolis, IN: Hackett, 1997.

Plutarch. *Moralia (Moral Essays).* Vol. 6. Translated by W. C. Helmbold. Loeb Classical Library 337. Cambridge: Harvard University Press, 1939.

Plutchik, Robert. *The Emotions.* Lanham, MD: University Press of America, 1991.

Rilke, Maria Rainer. *Selected Poems.* Oxford: Oxford University Press, 2011.

Riso, Don, and Russ Hudson. *The Wisdom of the Enneagram: The Complete Guide to Ppsychological and Spiritual Growth for the Nine Personality Types.* New York: Bantam, 1999.

Rohr, Richard. *Discovering the Enneagram: An Ancient Tool for a New Spiritual Journey.* New York: Crossroad, 1999.

Rufus, Musonius. *Lectures and Sayings.* CreateSpace, 2011.

Russell, Bertrand. *The Conquest of Happiness.* London: Routledge, 2008.

Rumi. *Selected Poems.* New York: Penguin, 2021.

Saraswati, Shantanand. *Good Company: An Anthology of Sayings, Stories, and Answers to Questions.* London: Study Society, 2017.

Seneca. *Moral Essays, Volume 1.* Translated by John W. Basore. Loeb Classical Library 214. Cambridge: Harvard University Press, 1928.

Sinek, Simon. *Start with Why: How Great Leaders Inspire Everyong to Take Action.* New York: Portfolio, 2009.

Sivananda, Sri Swami. *Conquest of Fear.* 5th ed. Shivananda Nagar, India: Divine Life Society, 1997. https://www.dlshq.org/download/conquest-of-fear/.

Spinoza, Benedict de. *Ethics.* Translated by Edwin Curley. New York: Penguin, 2005.

Svendsen, Lars. *A Philosophy of Fear.* Translated by John Irons. London: Reaktion, 2008.

Tagore, Rabindranath. *Collected Poems and Plays.* New Delhi: Rupa, 2002.

Wagner, Jerome. *Nine Lenses on the World: The Enneagram Perspective.* Evanston, IL: NineLens, 2010.

Wittgenstein, Ludwig. *Philosophical Investigations.* Translated by G. E. M. Anscombe et al. Malden, MA: Wiley-Blackwell, 2009.

———. *Tractatus Logico-Philosophicus.* Translated by D. F. Pears and B. F. McGuinness. London: Routledge, 2001.

Made in United States
North Haven, CT
22 December 2022

29854041R00078